INSIDE THE ANC

CICERO AND ROME

DAVID TAYLOR

Nelson

To Pamela

Thomas Nelson and Sons Ltd
Nelson House   Mayfield Road
Walton-on-Thames   Surrey
KT12 5PL   UK

51 York Place
Edinburgh
EH1 3JD   UK

Thomas Nelson (Hong Kong) Ltd
Toppan Building 10/F
22A Westlands Road
Quarry Bay   Hong Kong

Thomas Nelson Australia
102 Dodds Street
South Melbourne
Victoria 3205   Australia

Nelson Canada
1120 Birchmount Road
Scarborough Ontario
M1K 5G4   Canada

© David Taylor 1973

First published by Macmillan Education Ltd 1973
ISBN 0-333-14742-1

This edition published by Thomas Nelson and Sons Ltd 1992

ISBN 0-17-438507-2
NPN 9 8 7 6 5 4 3

Printed in Hong Kong.

Contents

	List of illustrations	7
1	Cicero and his World	11
2	Cicero, Pompey and the Senate	18
3	Cicero's Consulship	27
4	Cicero and the Triumvirate	34
5	From Exile to Civil War	48
6	Civil War and the Final Stand	70
	Appendix 1 Glossary of Latin terms	91
	Appendix 2 The Principal Characters	93
	Index	95

Acknowledgements

The Publishers wish to acknowledge the following sources of photographs:

Castello-die Aglie Fig 18; Giraudin, Paris Fig 17; Glyptotek, Copenhagen Fig 6; C. Hulsen Fig 31; El Laurenti Fig 25; The London Museum Fig 1; The Mansell Collection Figs 2, 3, 8, 9, 10, 17, 19, 21, 26, 27, 30; Mansell – Alinari Fig 12; Museo della Civilatà, Rome Figs 13, 22, 24; Musée Lapidaire Fig 29; Uffizzi, Florence Fig 28; Von Matt Figs 7, 11, 15.

The Publishers have made every effort to contact the copyright holders but, in cases where formal acknowledgement is not made, they will be pleased to make the necessary arrangements at the first opportunity.

List of Illustrations

		page
1	Roman writing materials	12
2	A schoolroom scene	14
3	Cicero	16
4	The Cursus Honorum	17
5	Italy	19
6	Pompey	20
7	Mithridates	24
8	The Roman Forum	25
9	Senators and Officials	29
10	Catiline listening to Cicero	31
11	Pompey the Great	37
12	A Roman Lady	38
13	Julius Caesar	42
14	Cicero's route into exile (April 58–August 57 BC)	49
15	A Roman married couple	50
16	A gladiator (retiarius, or net-fighter)	52
17	The hall in a town house	54
18	Julius Caesar	59
19	A two-horse carriage	61
20	Cilicia and Asia Minor	63
21	Legionaries building a camp	66
22	The legionary eagles and standards	71
23	The Roman Empire in the time of Cicero	75
24	Coin of Caesar struck by him while dictator	77

25 Reconstruction of the Temple of Julius Caesar   79

26 Coin of Brutus and the liberators   81
    (*reverse:* Cap of Liberty)

27 Brutus   81

28 Mark Antony   83

29 Octavian   87

30 Cicero   88

31 The public platform, where Cicero's head and hands
    were hung (*Reconstruction*)   90

General Editor's Preface

To get *inside* the Ancient World is no easy task. What is easy is to idealise the Greeks and Romans, or else to endow them unconsciously with our own conventional beliefs and prejudices. The aim of this series is to illuminate selected aspects of Antiquity in such a way as to encourage the reader to form his own judgement, from the inside, on the ways of life, culture and attitudes that characterised the Greco-Roman world. Where suitable, the books draw widely on the writings (freshly translated) of ancient authors in order to convey information and to illustrate contemporary views.

The topics in the series have been chosen both for their intrinsic interest and because of their central importance for the student who wishes to see the civilisations of Greece and Rome in perspective. The close interaction of literature, art, thought and institutions reveals the Ancient World in its totality. The opportunity should thus arise for making comparisons not only within that world, between Athens and Sparta, or Athens and Rome, but also between the world of Antiquity and our own.

The title 'Classical Studies' (or 'Classical Civilisation') is featuring more and more frequently in school timetables and in the prospectuses of universities. In schools, the subject is now studied at Advanced Level as well as at Key Stages 3 and 4. It is particularly for the latter courses that this new series has been designed; also, as in the case of this volume, as a helpful ancillary to the study of Latin and Greek in the sixth form and below. It is hoped that some of the books will interest students of English and History at these levels as well as the non-specialist reader.

The authors, who are teachers in schools or universities, have each taken an aspect of the Ancient World. They have tried not to give a romanticised picture but to portray, as vividly as possible, the Greeks and the Romans as they really were.

In *Cicero and Rome* David Taylor has taken the life of Marcus Tullius Cicero, a famous public speaker and politician of his day, as the focal point for a look at the world in which he lived and at the most powerful individuals of his period – those who shaped the dramatic and often violent events of the last years of the Roman Republic. After a brief account of Cicero's early years, his career is traced from the harsh dictatorship of Sulla (82 BC) to the orator's own death in the massacres of Mark Antony and the Second Triumvirate (43 BC).

One of the chief features of the book is the extensive use of Cicero's own words (and those of other Roman writers who described the period). It is particularly from the large number of private letters which Cicero wrote that a full picture can be gained both of the man himself and of his contemporaries. So, wherever possible, these letters – and especially those to his friend Atticus – have been used to tell the story of the period, and also as a starting-point for discussing the political issues and decisions which faced Cicero and others like him.

The lifetime of Cicero was an age full of political disagreement and controversy, often of a complicated and technical kind. Partly because of his own writings, something is known about most of the people involved in the struggles for power. Some of the debates can be followed in close detail: for example, the quarrels between the Senate and the most influential men outside the Senate, the *equites*.

Cicero and Rome does not attempt to deal with these problems exhaustively, nor does it wish to inundate the reader with a mass of Roman names to which it is impossible to fit faces. But it does give him an introduction to the principal characters who held the stage, and raises again some of the questions of right and wrong, wisdom and folly, which confronted men in Cicero's Rome.

MICHAEL GUNNINGHAM

I

Cicero and his World

Evidence for history

IN the year AD 4000, perhaps someone will be interested in finding out as much as he can about the Labour Party Government of England from 1964 to 1970, and about Harold Wilson, the Prime Minister at the time. He may well feel that he doesn't just want 'official' history, but wishes to look behind the scenes, to discover what really made him and his colleagues act as they did, and what their own thoughts were.

Where will he look for evidence? One place is Hansard, the word-by-word record of proceedings in Parliament. Or he will turn to later historians who described the period, and to newspapers of the day. Then there are the 'memoirs' of famous politicians. But better than all of this would be the discovery of something written privately by the men themselves. So he will be particularly delighted if a personal diary, or letters written to close friends, turn up.

If we want to find out what went on in the minds of politicians 2000 years ago, our aims are likely to be the same. But it will be a much harder task. From many important periods of ancient history, there is little or no written evidence surviving. It is extremely rare to find anything from so long ago which has the personal touch.

Cicero's letters

This is why the period of Roman history which this book deals with is so unusual. Marcus Tullius Cicero lived from 106 to 43 BC, and it is safe to say that more is known about him than about any man in ancient history. For one thing, he was the outstanding orator, or public speaker, of his day, and many of his most important speeches have been preserved. For another, he gained a high reputation as a writer on literary and philosophical subjects, which has allowed much of his writing to survive. But more than anything, we know Cicero from a vast collection of his private letters, and those of his friends (including most of the leading politicians

1. *Roman writing materials*

of his day) to him. Over 900 letters remain, and it is because of these that Cicero is quite without equal as a source of information and understanding about a dramatic period in Rome's history. Cicero was a tireless correspondent, and at times gives us not just a month-by-month summary of events in Rome, but a day-by-day commentary. The most important of all the letters are those to his close friend, Titus Pomponius Atticus. Cicero trusted him completely, and wrote to him frankly and without fear.

But the collection of letters which survives does not begin until he is about forty years old, so for earlier events we have to rely on other writers. The most useful of these is Plutarch, the Greek writer, who wrote life-histories of a number of the leading Romans of Cicero's age. He is not always accurate, and at times writes with bias, but the main outline of his work is trustworthy enough.

Cicero's background

The town of Arpinum, where Cicero was born on 3 January 106 BC, was about seventy miles to the south-east of Rome (see the map of Italy, p. 19). All inhabitants of Arpinum were also citizens of Rome—this was a right shared with many other Italian towns. This meant that Cicero was both a Roman and an Italian. For Rome was more than a capital city, it was *the* city. More than a city, it stood for the whole State, the *Respublica*.

An Italian who came to Rome was already at something of a social disadvantage. He could be sneered at for not being truly Roman—as happened to Cicero on one occasion, when he was called an 'immigrant'. However, it *was* possible to succeed at Rome if you came from a country-town like Arpinum. This very year, 106—from now on, all dates given will be taken to mean BC—a man from Arpinum (Caius Marius) was reaching the height of a brilliant military career. It brought him the highest political office, the consulship, not just once (as was normal) but seven times. Success was possible, then, but it was not easy. Cicero's own family were well-off, respectable people, but none of them had had a place in the most important political body, the Senate. The Senate consisted largely of a number of influential families (the *nobiles*) with long and proud histories. It was jealous about whom it allowed to join its ranks.

The name Cicero

Cicero's name, well enough known in Arpinum, was unfamiliar in Rome. Plutarch tells the following story. Even if not strictly true, it gives the right idea:

> *Cicer* is the Latin word for a chick-pea, and one of Cicero's ancestors must have got the name because of a dent or nick in the end of his nose, like the opening in the chick-pea. Cicero himself is said to have given a lively reply to his friends on one occasion. When he first entered politics, they said he ought to drop or change the name. He said that he would do his best to make the name Cicero more famous than names like Scaurus or Catulus. [Plutarch, *Life of Cicero* 1]

In this he certainly succeeded—how many people today know anything about Scaurus or Catulus?

His education

Before Cicero could think about politics and the Senate, he had a long education and a hard training to pass through. He seems to have done well at school, at least if this story of Plutarch's is anything to go by:

> He had quite remarkable ability as a boy. In fact, he got such a reputation among the others that their fathers used to come to school with them just to see this Cicero. [Plutarch, *Life of Cicero* 2]

Cicero took well to the studies in literature and philosophy which were such an important part of Roman education. But his education did not

2. *A schoolroom scene*

end in the classroom—he had to go on to study law and oratory, and also undergo military training. The army was not really to Cicero's taste, but it brought him into contact with a man called Sulla, who became the most powerful figure in Rome at the time when Cicero was completing his own preparations for entering politics.

The rule of Sulla: 82-79

After a period of about 20 years which had involved Rome in a series of wars, both at home and abroad, Sulla was called in by the Senate to settle the crisis. The title he took was *dictator*, which was an appointment made in emergencies granting one man powers greater even than the consuls', but for a limited time. He obtained the position because of his own military strength.

The Senate and its opponents

Sulla believed that the Senate was the only body fit to govern Rome. Recently, however, its power had been threatened, and even bypassed, by certain politicians. Sulla realised that such men had a legal way to get round the Senate, in the office of the tribunes (*tribuni plebis*). These officers were allowed to pass their laws straight to the Assembly of the people, instead of taking them through the usual channel, the Senate. The rights of the tribunes dated back to the time when they had been set up to protect the interests of the plebeians, at that time the less privileged class of citizens in comparison with the patricians. In order to stop tribunes acting against the Senate, Sulla now took away these rights. His other measures were also designed to secure the Senate from outside attack, and the threat of military power deciding events. But the most obviously significant feature of the dictatorship was Sulla's so-called 'proscriptions'—lists of 'wanted' men who were regarded by Sulla as dangerous to his new constitution. Large numbers of high-ranking Romans found themselves on the lists, often for no apparent reason. They were killed by Sulla's men.

Even allowing for the fact that such events as these tend to be exaggerated afterwards to make them appear still more atrocious, it was quite clearly a time of widespread horror, fear and uncertainty. Romans remembered it for many years. It underlined the fact that legalised violence was now a part of Roman public life, and for the next fifty years, it was never far beneath the surface.

Cicero the orator

The period of the proscriptions coincided with Cicero's emergence in the law-courts. It was as an orator that he was at first to make his mark on Rome, and in the courts that his name began to become known. In 80, he made a speech in defence of a man called Roscius. As Sulla had passed a law making the juries of the law-courts consist only of senators, Cicero would be speaking before the very people whom he was so anxious to join.

It was a tricky case. Many more experienced lawyers had turned it down, because it involved making an accusation against one of Sulla's close supporters. It would be dangerous for Cicero to say anything to offend the dictator. He managed the task skilfully, winning much popularity among the senators, while taking care not to criticise Sulla directly:

> You must realise, gentlemen, as I have reminded you already, that all these offences were committed without Sulla knowing about them. . . .
> You would like to think that in this case I am attacking Sulla, but I am not. . . .
> The Roman people triumphed under the skilful command of the brilliant and successful Sulla. . . . [Cicero, *Pro Roscio* passim]

By such remarks as these, Cicero managed to stay on the right side of Sulla, and still made some damaging criticisms of the way Sulla's rule worked.

3. *Cicero*

Improving his art

From this point on, Cicero's career was launched. After Sulla's retire-
ment and death in 78, he was almost ready to make his bid for entry into
the Senate. But in the meantime he was not idle. He had gone to Greece
and learned a great deal about the art of oratory. (It was also here that he
met Atticus.) A story of Plutarch's reveals how well he learned his skills:

In Rhodes, he was taught oratory by the Son of Molon, Apollonius. . . . It was said that Apollonius, who did not know Latin, asked Cicero to speak in Greek. Cicero was glad to do so, because he thought this would make it easier to have his mistakes corrected. So he made a speech, and when it was over, all who had heard it were falling over themselves with praises. But Apollonius had not appeared very excited while listening, and when Cicero finished, he sat there for a long time, deep in thought. Cicero was upset by this, but finally Apollonius said to him, Cicero, I must congratulate you. It was an astonishing performance. The reason I am sad is for the sake of Greece. All we had left to us was our culture and eloquence. Now it looks as though Rome, through you, is going to take these away from us too. [Plutarch, *Life of Cicero* 4]

The task before him

In 77, Cicero returned to Rome. As we follow him on his path through the Senate to the consulship, we should bear in mind that there were precise rules governing the way in which offices in the Senate could be held, which Sulla had reinforced. Normally, though with important exceptions, these were obeyed absolutely. The chart below shows how the *cursus honorum* (ladder of offices) operated, and there is further information about the various offices in Appendix 1:

THE CURSUS HONORUM

Minimum age		Number elected annually
43	CONSUL	Two
40	PRAETOR	Eight
37	(AEDILE)	Four
30	QUAESTOR	Twenty

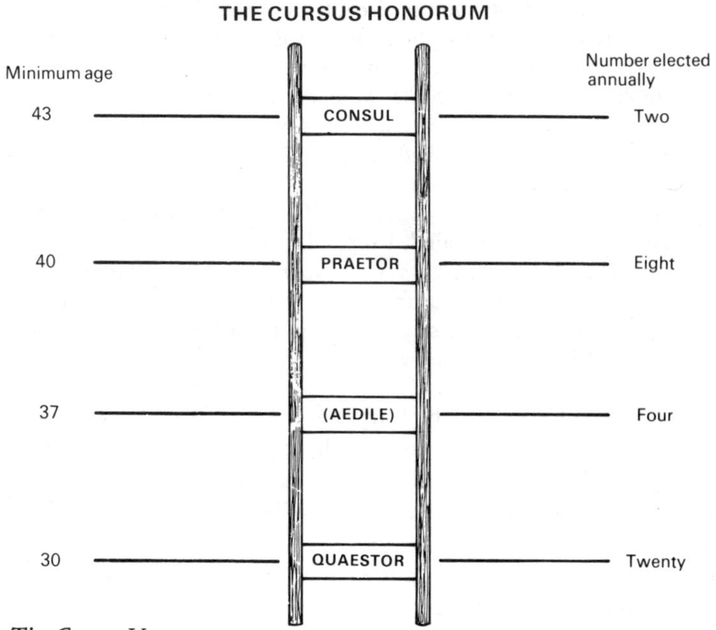

4. *The Cursus Honorum*

B

2

Cicero, Pompey and the Senate

The quaestorship

When in 76 Cicero, now almost thirty years old, stood for the position of quaestor, a lot was at stake. He had gained considerable support from his success in the law-courts, but could not know whether this was enough to gain for the unknown name from Arpinum a place on the Senate roll. It turned out that it was: Cicero was duly elected, and his task was to assist the governor of the province of Sicily, based at Lilybaeum (see map of Italy, page 19). Cicero worked hard, and was pleased with the results. But he showed that he could laugh at himself too:

> To tell the truth, I actually thought at the time that people at Rome were talking about nothing except my quaestorship. . . . So when I left Sicily I thought that the people of Rome would be eager to place the whole world at my feet. On the way home I called in by chance at Puteoli; all the best people were there—it was the height of the season. But you could have knocked me down with a feather when someone came up and asked me when I had left Rome, and what the latest news from the city was. I replied: 'As a matter of fact, I'm on my way home from my province.' 'Oh, of course', he said, 'Africa, wasn't it?' 'Sicily, actually', I replied, pretty annoyed by now. Then someone, with the air of a real expert, broke in, 'Good heavens, didn't you realise that our friend here has been quaestor at *Syracuse?*' That did it. I gave up, swallowed my pride, and lost myself in the crowds. [Cicero, *Pro Plancio* 64-6]

Cicero went on to say that he learned a very valuable lesson from this incident: the important thing, as far as his career was concerned, was not that people should *hear* about his deeds, but they must actually *see* him. After this, he added, 'I lived in sight of the Roman people, and was never away from the Forum.'

But even if not everyone realised how important this year was for Cicero, he himself knew it. He was now a senator, and unless he committed some moral or criminal outrage, he was there for life.

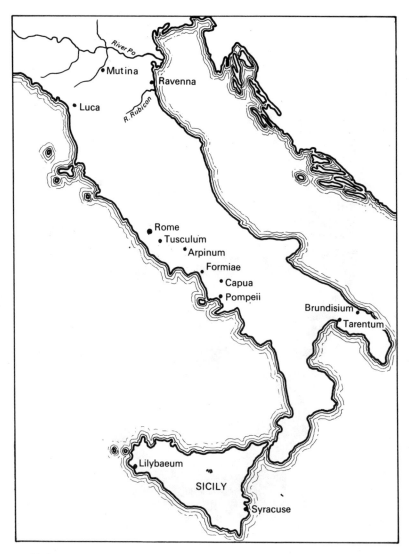

5. *Italy*

Pompey's consulship

Cicero returned from Sicily to find a Rome full of political unrest and agitation. Sulla's attempts to bring stability to Rome had not been successful; in the space of ten years, almost all his measures had been undone. For one thing, the tribunes had regained their old powers, the right to pass laws to the people's Assembly, and the power of the veto.

6. *Pompey*

But the most serious breach occurred when Pompey (Gnaeus Pompeius Magnus), seized the consulship of 70, together with the rich and powerful Crassus. Pompey was born in the same year as Cicero—106. He was therefore seven years younger than the required age of forty-three. Also, he had used his immense military power to gain this position, as he had previously gained a number of important military commands in a way which was strictly illegal.

The trial of Verres

The year 70 was again crucial for Cicero. One of the things that still remained in the Senate's control was the composition of the law-courts. But here too they were being vigorously attacked. The opposition argued that it was wrong to allow a court consisting entirely of senators to try cases where their own number were being charged (often by people not in the Senate). This was particularly serious, they claimed, in cases involving provincial governors accused of abusing their position. A case like this now brought the question into focus. Verres had recently been governor of Sicily (where Cicero himself had been quaestor), and was accused by the Sicilians of extortion. (He had, it was stated, stolen a number of famous art treasures, and generally made himself and friends rich at the expense of the inhabitants.)

Cicero was now standing for the aedileship—the next rung up the ladder—and this made the case all the more important for him. He applied to become prosecutor, and got the position. Then he proceeded to amass evidence, working with great zeal. There was plenty of evidence to be found, and it was damning. Cicero's speed and urgency were too much for Verres. After Cicero had delivered the first of the speeches he had prepared, Verres abandoned his defence and left Rome.

More had been at stake than the fate of Verres, as Cicero saw:

> 'In this trial, you, the judges, will be sitting in judgement on the man accused; but you yourselves will be on trial before the Roman people.' [Cicero, *in Verrem* I 47]

What Cicero meant by this was that if Verres was acquitted, it would be a condemnation of the Senate, for an irresponsible and corrupt attitude to the courts. Cicero knew this, and said in his speech:

> 'At this time the Roman people are searching for a new type of man to serve in the law-courts. A law has recently been proposed which will provide new courts, and new judges.' [Cicero, *in Verrem* II 177]

The Equites and the courts

The pressure for the change came from the *equites*. Wealthy men, often with strong financial interests in the provinces, they had emerged in Rome as a force to be reckoned with in politics. They were not senators, but often had very powerful support within the Senate (for example, Crassus). Before Sulla's legislation, they had been in control of the courts for a time.

Now, if Verres was not condemned, there would be strong grounds for giving the courts back to the *equites*. In the end, a compromise solution was reached. The courts were to be composed of three groups, equal in number—one from the Senate, one from the *equites*, and a third group, with interests very similar to the *equites*. Sulla would not have liked it, but the new courts did recognise that the *equites* could not be overlooked, and that the Senate could not have unbridled power to do as it wished.

Cicero and Pompey

The year of Verres' trial brought Cicero and Pompey into close contact for the first time. The connexion was to continue for twenty years, with important effects for Rome. Pompey and Cicero were the same age, but while Cicero worked his way up the political ladder carefully, reaching office at the earliest legal date allowed, Pompey did not, as we saw earlier.

Cicero realised now—and never in fact forgot—the importance of Pompey. To a man whose prospects for promotion depended on securing support from as many influential persons and groups as possible, the political friendship of Pompey could be invaluable. It was no doubt largely because of his brilliant attack on Verres that Cicero had now acquired a reputation which could not be ignored. If he was to progress still further than the position of aedile (which he held in 69), he would have to play his cards very carefully. He decided that Pompey was the man to follow, and the decision paid off.

Pompey's command against the pirates

In 67 Pompey, who had been searching since his consulship in 70 for a chance to increase his prestige by fresh military successes, got the opportunity he wanted. The Mediterranean Sea had been plagued for many years by pirates, and a tribune, Gabinius, passed a law giving Pompey extraordinary powers throughout the Mediterranean, and for fifty miles inland, for the purpose of clearing the sea of this menace. Pompey carried out the task with great efficiency and thoroughness. The same year, Cicero stood successfully for the praetorship of 66—the next step up the ladder.

66: Cicero as praetor

During his praetorship, Cicero delivered one of his most important speeches, politically speaking. Pompey had reached the Black Sea, while clearing the Mediterranean. There was some reason to suggest that the pirate nuisance had been made worse by King Mithridates, an Asian king who had troubled Rome in wars covering about twenty years. In 66, taking advantage of his position and success over the pirates, Pompey used another tribune, Manilius, to propose that he should be given the military command in Asia. This bill, like that of Gabinius in 67, was carried despite considerable opposition within the Senate. They both show how important the powers of the tribune could be to an ambitious man who was not prepared to give in to the wishes of the Senate.

As praetor, Cicero must have been very hesitant about siding with Pompey against the wishes of the influential leaders of the Senate—but other factors were involved. The situation in Asia (the war was beginning to look as if it might never finish) certainly seemed to call for a really top-ranking general. Moreover, Asia was a province where many Roman businessmen had very strong interests, which were threatened considerably by the wars. Cicero himself came from this class of financial businessmen (the *equites*), and they looked on him as their spokesman for their interests, particularly with regard to the collection of taxes in the province.

There were, then, issues which made Cicero prepared to risk offending leading senators, if he could secure the wider support which a speech on Pompey's behalf could bring. And when he had decided to speak for Pompey, he did so with great vigour:

> 'Consider the case of Pompey, for whom Catulus does not want any new precedent to be established; think what a number of innovations have already been introduced for him, and with the full backing of Catulus.
>
> What could be so unprecedented as that a young man, holding no office, should raise an army at a time of crisis in the state? But he raised one. Or that he should command it? But he commanded it. Or that his command should be crowned with success? But it was. . . . All the innovations made in individual cases from the beginning of our history are fewer than those we have witnessed in the case of this single man. And all these remarkable and revolutionary precedents have been established for Pompey by the influence of Catulus and other distinguished men of similar status.' [Cicero, *de imperio Gn. Pompei* 60–3]

Cicero cleverly argued that Catulus (one of his leading opponents on this issue) and the rest of the Senate had been prepared to bend the constitution before—recognising that Pompey was quite outstanding in his military abilities—so why should they not do so now? It was a hazardous line to take—and surely Cicero would not have been too happy to think of what it might imply: that the constitution could be twisted or ignored whenever convenient. Later events were to prove that the rules and principles of constitutional government *could* be flouted like this, and

Cicero was horrified at the results. But at this time, no doubt, he did not think that such a situation could arise, and was more concerned with presenting a case which he thought would be useful in the short term—useful for Rome, for the tax-collectors, and also for himself: he already had at least one eye on the possibility of standing for consulship.

Cicero's campaign for the consulship

Pompey obtained the command against the old king, Mithridates, and was away from Rome for the next four years. While he was absent,

7. *Mithridates*

Cicero started to think seriously about being consul. His preparations were very thorough. Plutarch puts it like this:

> He decided that . . . a statesman should not be lazy or indifferent when it came to knowing his fellow-citizens. So he trained himself to memorise names, and also to get to know whereabouts in the city all the important people lived, and where their country houses were, and who were their friends and neighbours. In this way it became easy for him to name and point out the estates and houses of his friends, wherever in Italy he was travelling. [Plutarch, *Life of Cicero* 7]

A document has survived from Roman times known as 'A short Guide to Electioneering', and it contains advice to Cicero on the steps he must take to make his campaign effective. (It may well have been written by his younger brother, Quintus, though this is uncertain.) The kind of advice it gives is much along the lines of the extract from Plutarch above; and

8. *The Roman Forum*

it stresses the importance of 'friends' (the Latin word *amici* perhaps means 'supporters' as well) of all types of men:

> 'You must have in your thoughts and memory a list in which each town in Italy is entered, in such a way that there is no single town, settlement or province—in fact, no place at all in Italy—in which you have not gained a sufficiently firm foothold. Search out and discover men in every area; get to know them, visit them, strengthen their loyalty, make sure that in their own vicinity they are campaigning for you, and pleading your cause as though they themselves were the candidate.' [*Commentariolum Petitionis* 30-1]

There is obviously some similarity between the way in which Cicero conducted his campaign, and election methods used nowadays—the basic aim is to get yourself known and supported as widely as possible, even among people who really know nothing about you at all.

Advice to a 'New Man'

It was the fact that Cicero was what the Romans called a *novus homo*, a 'new man', which the 'Short Guide to Electioneering' stresses most strongly. (New men were contrasted in the Senate with the *nobiles*, or nobles—families which had included in their ranks a consul.) The guide starts by saying that Cicero is in an excellent position so far as qualities for the consulship go. But, it continues:

'Although natural talent is most important, in a matter which lasts only a few months it can, it seems, be defeated by fraud. Consider what city this is, what you are seeking, who you are. Almost every day as you go down to the Forum, you must bear this in mind: "I am a new man. I am seeking the consulship. This is Rome." The fact that you are a new man will be made considerably less hard by the reputation of your oratory; for oratory has always brought great distinction. A man who is thought worthy to be the advocate of men of consular rank cannot be considered unworthy of the consulship. . . . See that people know how many friends you have and what sort of men they are. For what new men have possessed the advantages which you have? You have all the tax-collectors, many men of every class whom you have defended, and a large and constant circle of friends in daily attendance. Take care to hold on to these advantages by giving these men advice, by seeking their help and by using all possible means to ensure that those who are indebted to you realise that this will be the best chance they will ever have of repaying their debt.' [*Commentariolum Petitionis* 1-4]

So although Cicero *was* a new man, he was a new man with a difference. His position had been transformed by his public speaking, which had made him almost without peer in the law-courts, and he received wide support from Italians of all kinds.

3
Cicero's Consulship

Cicero's success

All Cicero's careful preparation paid off. In the first important speech he delivered in 63, this is what he had to say for himself:

> 'I am the first "new man" made consul for a very long time—I could almost say the first within living memory. With me as leader, you have broken open the stronghold which the *nobiles* had protected so carefully, and guarded so closely. You have shown that for the future you wish its gates to be open to those who deserve entry. . . . And nothing could be more splendid or glorious than this fact: when you elected me consul, you didn't do so silently, relying on the fact that the voting-boxes would indicate your free choice. No, you elected me openly, you raised your voices to indicate your goodwill to me and your enthusiastic support for my cause.' [Cicero, *de lege agraria* II 3-4]

His election was certainly a convincing one, and it is perhaps not surprising in the event that he should have given himself a fairly generous pat on the back. (Modesty about one's own success was not considered so much of a virtue in Roman times as it is today, and in Cicero it is conspicuous only by its absence!) He went on, in the speech quoted from above, to speak as follows:

> 'I realise that I owe my election, in which I defeated men of the highest nobility, not to being supported just by a group of powerful men, or to the wide influence of a small minority. I owe it to the will of the whole Roman people. So it is necessary for me to be seen to be on the side of the people—both during my year of office and in the rest of my life.' [Cicero, *de lege agraria* II 7]

But, Cicero argued, there were a number of people who called themselves *populares* (on the side of the people) who were really aiming to destroy the State for their own ends, and were bent on tyranny and revolution.

'Since I could see this clearly. . . . I said, speaking in the Senate, that I should be a people's consul (*consul popularis*). For what is so precious to the people as peace . . . or harmony in the State?' [Cicero, *de lege agraria* II 9]

The political groupings

(a) Populares

At this point, it would be useful to look a little more closely at the political issues at Rome at this time. In Cicero's writings, he refers frequently to a group of people called *populares*. Although there were no fixed parties, such as our 'Conservative' and 'Labour' parties, there was a grouping of men who could loosely be described as the popular party—the *populares*. What this meant was that they preferred to pass laws in the popular assemblies rather than use the Senate. Pompey's use of tribunes was typical of this. Why they preferred to do this is a more complicated question: sometimes they were aiming at some kind of social reform which they felt would be disliked by the Senate; at other times it was simply an attempt at a short cut. Although Cicero had supported Pompey in 66, and liked to be thought of as a *consul popularis*, he was not in favour of such a course in general. He believed in the Senate, as the most effective and important part of the Republic. So, in calling himself a *popularis*, without wishing to be identified with the reforms associated with the *populares*, he was in a sense trying to eat his cake and still have it.

(b) Optimates

There was a rival group, who were referred to as the *optimates* (those on the side of the 'best' people.) Like Cicero, these men had a very high regard for the Senate, but unlike him they were often inclined to think that *only* the Senate's interests should be taken seriously, and so they pursued policies which Cicero at times regarded as short-sighted. Their opposition to Pompey's command was an example of this. The *optimates* very much wished to retain power in their own circles. Even within the Senate, there were degrees of importance. The most important people were those who had been consuls (called *consulares*, or consulars), and their influence and control of affairs was very great: *optimates* wanted to keep it that way— they were therefore inclined to be 'conservatives', in that they wished to conserve the structure in which their families—the smallish group of noble households—and their supporters, could dominate the political scene. They were frightened (with some reason) of the development of power outside their ranks.

9. *Senators and Officials*

The fear of revolution

Cicero probably owed his success, apart from his skill in the law-courts and the wide support he had in Italy, to the fact that the *optimates* regarded him as fairly 'safe'. Although he styled himself a *popularis*, it must have been obvious to the leading senators that he was not a man to side with revolutionary ideas, and was too concerned about staying on the right side of the *nobiles*, whose ranks he had so recently joined, ever to do anything wildly 'popular'. He shared their fear of revolutionary elements, and in the event was to have an outstanding opportunity to preserve the Republic against enemies within.

Catiline

In his speech at the start of his consulship, Cicero had spoken about the desire of the people for peace. He had in mind recent events which had caused much alarm, and were continuing to do so. In 65 there had been a threat of revolution, and one of the men whose name had been linked with the plot was still very much alive and kicking. His name was Lucius Sergius Catilina (generally known as Catiline), and in 64 he had stood against Cicero for the consulship, without success. He was determined on

29

power, and was preparing for the elections of July 63, hoping to be consul in 62.

Catiline was not a lone voice. There were plenty of people who were far from satisfied with the government. Particularly it was those, from all classes, who were in a bad way economically—and there were very many of them. Men of Catiline's wealthy background had often got into debt through extravagance, but there were large numbers, often unemployed, who simply could not make ends meet. One of Catiline's promises was to cancel all debts, and in this way he won a very considerable following. At one time this included a number of senators whose sympathies tended to lie on the *popularis* side.

Cicero had been finding it difficult to persuade the Senate that Catiline was a real danger to the State, and now he used shock tactics against his enemy. At the elections for next year's consulship, he turned up wearing a breastplate, visible beneath his toga, and accompanied by a strong bodyguard.

His idea worked, in that Catiline failed yet again. But it was not the end of the threat. Catiline now resorted to more extreme measures:

> Since secret plans had brought him only defeat and disgrace, he had no choice but open war. . . . At Rome he had several plans on the go at the same time. He was intending to kill the consuls, organise the burning of buildings, and occupy important strategic points with armed men. He went round armed himself, urging his followers to do the same. [Sallust, *The Conspiracy of Catiline* 27]

The Catilinarian Conspiracy

While Catiline was making his various plans, Cicero was far from idle, and he had his spies out. Matters reached a head in late October 63. Catiline had arranged that he himself would stay at Rome. This would enable him to be the central organiser, but it also had a good effect in helping him to bluff his way through, and avoid suspicion. His agent, a man called Manlius, was to lead and unite armed forces outside Rome, ready to move in on the city.

News of this reached Cicero. On 21 October he spoke to the Senate and because he was able to produce details about Manlius' likely action, the Senate passed the *Consultum Ultimum*, their 'Ultimate Decree', the measure which gave Cicero the power to take military action. Cicero acted. Defences were manned both inside the city and outside, and troops were raised. But Catiline did not give in, nor did he appear worried. He could afford to do this because Cicero simply did not have enough proof against him. So both Cicero and Catiline played a waiting game, Cicero hoping that his military organisation would force Catiline to come out into the open, and preferably leave Rome to take command, Catiline perhaps hoping to convince the Senate that there was nothing to worry about, and that Cicero was making a lot of fuss about nothing. On the night of 6 November, another secret meeting was held by the leading conspirators. Cicero had to be removed. Lentulus, a fellow-conspirator, was to be put in charge of operations in Rome, while Catiline himself would now leave the city. This is how they planned to put the strategy into operation:

> They decided to go to the house of Cicero later in the night, together with a band of armed men, and to be admitted to the house by pretending they were making a ceremonial morning visit. After this, they would take him by surprise and assassinate him in his own house, before he could defend himself. But a man called Curius, who realised the danger of death that the consul was in, hurried to warn him of the trap. So when they arrived, they found the door barred against them, and failed completely. [Sallust, *The Conspiracy of Catiline* 28]

On 8 November, Cicero summoned the Senate again. They met in a temple of Jupiter, instead of the Senate House, because this was easier to guard. Catiline still braved it out, and took his seat, to hear Cicero pronounce what is known as his First Catilinarian speech:

> 'How long, Catiline, in the name of God, will you push our patience to the limit? How long will your mad schemes defy our will? Is there

10. *Catiline listening to Cicero*

no end to your unrestrained insolence? Can nothing stop you in your crazy career? . . . Don't you realise that all your plans are known, that your plots cannot prevail?' [Cicero, *in Catilinam* 1 1]

It was a stirring speech, but for all that, Cicero still lacked really crushing evidence. He stated at one point that he could have had Catiline arrested and executed, but knew that the Ultimate Decree did not in fact give him such power.

But although Catiline could—and did—reply, he could stay in Rome no longer. Cicero was still alive, and organising Roman forces with ferocious energy. If he did not join them, Catiline knew that his forces could easily lose heart. So he left, complete with the trappings of an army commander. Cicero was triumphant. In the Senate the next day he started his second speech: 'He's gone, got away; escaped, broken out.' He explained the whole plot, and his arrangements to meet it. Later in the month the news reached Rome that Catiline had arrived in the camp of Manlius, claiming to be a Roman commander. The Senate outlawed him, along with Manlius.

This was far from the end, though. The next step was to deal with those of Catiline's forces in Rome, under Lentulus. Lentulus was in fact praetor, and care needed to be taken in dealing with a man of his rank. But evidence was brought against him, and the Senate voted that he should resign his office and be kept under house-arrest. At this point, according to Sallust:

> The fact that the plot had been revealed caused the lower classes to change their minds completely. They now cursed the conspiracy and praised Cicero's plans highly. They had at first been attracted to the idea of war, seeking for political change through it, but now showed joy and excitement, as though rescued from slavery. [Sallust, *The Conspiracy of Catiline* 48]

This action had taken place on 3 December. For the next two days there was a debate about the prisoners' fate. On the night of 4 December, there had been an unsuccessful attempt to free them. Two possibilities were proposed—one that they should be put to death, the other (from Julius Caesar) that they should be kept securely in prison. Cicero spoke (his Fourth Catilinarian) on the side of the death-penalty:

> 'Therefore, gentleman of the Senate, for your own safety and that of the Roman people, for your wives and children, your hearths and altars, the shrines and temples of the gods, your own houses and homes in the city, government and freedom, and the protection of the whole of Italy and the Republic, you must be daring and firm in your

vote. You have a consul who is not afraid to carry out your orders; so long as this consul is alive, he has the power to defend and safeguard your decision, whatever it is.' [Cicero, *in Catilinam* IV 24]

The debate continued for a time, with a number of speakers expressing opinions on Caesar's side. Then came the turn of Marcus Porcius Cato, a young politician who was to be one of the leading representatives of the point of view of the *optimates* for nearly twenty years. He sided with Cicero, and turned the tide of the debate. Cicero put the motion again, in the terms which Cato had proposed, and it was passed. Cicero supervised the execution of the prisoners in person. He returned to the Senate with the announcement, in a single word, '*Vixere*'—'They have had their lives'. It was 5 December 63, Cicero's great day—what he afterwards referred to as the 'immortal glory of the 5th'.

The Final Stages

The news of Lentulus' death soon reached the camp of Catiline, and more of his support now dropped away. Catiline himself hoped to escape to Gaul, but was cut off by the Republican forces, and forced to join battle. Both sides contained picked Roman troops, and Catiline's spirit in this final action was fierce and determined. The decisive move came when Petreius, the leader of the State's forces, threw his crack cohort against Catiline's centre, and inflicted heavy losses, following this up with two flank attacks. Sallust's description of the final stages goes like this:

> When Catiline saw that his army was routed, and that he had only a handful of men left, he thought of his birth and his former high position, and plunged into the thick of the enemy line, fighting on until he had been pierced time and time again. After the battle was over, it was possible to see the desperate courage with which Catiline's men had fought. Practically everyone lay dead in the very position which he had occupied for the battle. A few in the centre, where the cohort of Petreius had broken through, had given ground a little way, but even these fell facing the enemy, their wounds on the front of their bodies. Catiline was discovered a long distance ahead of his forces, among the dead of the enemy. He was still breathing faintly, and on his face was the expression which had been his throughout life—one of bold arrogance. Not a single freeborn citizen from the whole of his army was captured, either in battle or in flight; they had not spared their own lives any more than those of their opponents. [Sallust, *The Conspiracy of Catiline* 60-1]

4
Cicero and the Triumvirate

The concordia ordinum

The year of his consulship, then, finished on a high note for Cicero. Although the execution of the Catilinarians had been opposed by influential men in the Senate, and although there was a real doubt about the strict legality of the action, Cicero had no reason at the time to fear that these events would bring him anything other than praise and glory. As has been seen, he was not a man to be modest about his achievements, and he shortly began to talk, in public and private, about the time when he saved the Republic—to such an extent that one Roman writer said of him that his praise of himself was 'not undeserved, but interminable'.

But, to be fair, Cicero was not only delighted with his victory over Catiline because of his own glory. As we have watched Cicero's career, we have seen that his constant wish was to gain support not only from the *nobiles*, but also from Romans and Italians outside the Senate. This was no doubt partly because he believed this would be the best way for him to succeed, but there was also a political ideal. It gained expression in what in the coming years he often called the *concordia ordinum*—'the unity of the orders'. By this, Cicero meant a working together of the Senate with the *equites*, embracing the whole of Italy. What so delighted him about the defeat of Catiline was that all these forces had rallied to his standard. Disagreements and quarrels had been forgotten: the Republic had united to withstand a common foe. The fullest expression of this idea is found in Cicero's Fourth Catilinarian Speech: ·

> 'I have support from men of every rank, every class, every age. . . . At last, for the first time in this city's history, a cause has arisen which has united the whole nation. (Apart from those who have decided to pull the people to destruction along with themselves, since they know that they must die and do not want to die alone. These men, however, I am glad to ignore and overlook. I don't think of them as disreputable citizens: they are the worst possible public enemies.) But when I think of the rest—I can't find the words to praise

them. They have given proof of their united concern for the common safety and glory of Rome by their massed support, their enthusiasm, their bravery. The *equites* may be below you in rank and influence, gentleman of the Senate, but they are showing a patriotism which it is up to you to try to match. After so many years·of struggling, the crisis which now faces us has brought them into harmony and agreement with your own ranks. If this harmony, brought about in my consulship, can survive for ever in the Republic, then we shall never again see the State torn apart by civil war and strife.' [Cicero, *in Catilinam* IV 14-15]

Cicero proceeded to go through all the classes of citizens, showing that there was no one, however poor, who did not join in the fight against Catiline. But there is no doubt that it was the harmony between the Senate and *equites* which he was really concerned about. In the coming years he gave no indication that he was in the least bit interested in the unprivileged classes in the Republic. What he *was* worried about was that some of the *optimates*, with whose point of view he was basically sympathetic, seemed to be quite oblivious to the need to reconcile the *equites*. In studying the events of the next ten years, it is worth considering whether Cicero's ideal did represent a real alternative to the course which Roman politics actually took.

Pompey's reactions to Cicero's achievement

One of the first effects of Cicero's new-found optimism was that he wrote a long letter to Pompey in which he told him all about his success in rescuing the Republic from the threat of Catiline. When Pompey replied, it was obvious that he had not reacted as favourably as Cicero hoped. The original letter to Pompey, and Pompey's reply, have not survived. But the next in the series has come down to us, and this is what it says:

To Pompey, in Asia Minor   Rome, Summer 62

'I hope that all is well with you and your army. Along with everyone else, I was extremely pleased to read your official letter. Because of my confidence in you, I have always affirmed that there would be peace in Asia, and the signs are good. . . .

Turning to your private letter to me, I can assure you it was very welcome—even though it gave only a slight indication of your friendship. . . . But to put it frankly (as my nature and our relationship demands), there was something I missed in your letter, and I'll tell you what it was. I was rather expecting some words of congratulation from you for what I achieved—both because we are friends and for the sake of the State. I imagine the reason you said nothing was the fear of offending someone. But let me tell you that my actions to save the Republic have been approved by the opinion of the whole world. When you return to Rome you will realise that I have acted so wisely and courageously that you will be pleased to associate with me in political matters and in private friendship. You are a far greater man than Scipio Africanus, and I am not that much inferior to *his* chief adviser, Laelius.' [Cicero, *ad Familiares* v 7]

This letter raises a number of interesting points. For a start it gives an idea about Cicero's character, and the way he thought about his consulship. It also shows what he thought his role in politics should be. He was no doubt hoping that Pompey would return from Asia to become the head of the grand alliance between Senate and *equites*, and that he would act as his adviser on political matters. (Pompey, like Scipio Africanus, was above all a *military* hero.) But we can also see that Pompey was not pleased with Cicero for some reason, and it is interesting to think why this might be.

Reasons for Pompey's attitude

Various explanations have been attempted, but the most likely seems to be that Pompey felt that Cicero had neglected him during the Asian wars. From the praises which Cicero had sung on his behalf in 66, Pompey must have hoped that the orator would use his influence to keep the name 'Pompey' on everyone's lips. In fact this had not happened. Cicero had been bound up in his own affairs, and Pompey must have sensed that some of the popularity and influence that he had enjoyed before leaving for Asia was now slipping away from him. It is not surprising that he was cautious about Cicero's glorious deeds, and uncertain where they left his own position.

Pompey's return from Asia

This same caution was reflected in Pompey's actions when he returned home from the East. There could be no doubt that he had handled the war thoroughly, even if Mithridates was fast running out of steam by the time he arrived. There has been much speculation about why Pompey did not try a military takeover when he returned. Perhaps the best short answer is that it was not in his nature. He was not primarily a politician, and the idea of a military dictatorship probably had little appeal. When he came back to Italy, he simply disarmed his legions outside the city, and asked the Senate to grant what he needed to complete the war: land for his veterans, and the Senate's formal agreement to the settlement he proposed for the East. His aim seems to have been to prove to the *optimates* that he was no dangerous revolutionary, and to win their trust and backing.

11. *Pompey the Great*

Having decided against an attempt to gain his requirements by force, Pompey was forced to play a waiting game. We know Cicero's reactions to his homecoming, for it is at this point, the beginning of 61, that a series of letters to his friend Atticus begins:

'To turn to that great friend of yours . . . he is making out that he's really fond of me, embraces me and is full of affection: in public, that is—secretly he's jealous of me, and can't hide the fact. The man lacks all refinement, and he's not at all straightforward; there's no generosity in his political actions, no honour, no courage, no frankness.' [Cicero, *ad Atticum* 1 13]

A fortnight later, on 13 February 61, he reports:

'I've already described to you Pompey's first speech in public—it didn't give the poor any hope, nor any encouragement to scoundrels; the rich were dissatisfied, and loyal citizens found it lacking in substance. All in all, it fell flat.' [Cicero, *ad Att.* 1 14]

Cicero appears to have decided the occasion was ripe for one of his own great speeches:

'As for my own speech—good Lord, how I laid it on now that I had Pompey in my audience! . . . In short, I was cheered and cheered. I was speaking about the dignity of the Senate, harmony with the *equites*, the common purpose of the whole of Italy, the dying embers of the conspiracy, falling prices, and the establishment of peace. You know how I can really let loose when I'm on those themes! . . . The state of affairs at Rome is this, then: the Senate is quite ideal—nothing could be imagined more solid, serious and full of spirit.' [*Ibid.*]

Cicero was in optimistic vein. But meanwhile the placid surface was ruffled slightly by a rather bizarre event.

The Clodius scandal

In December 62, a band of noble ladies were meeting in honour of the *Bona Dea* (Good Goddess), in the house of Julius Caesar, then praetor. Men were strictly banned, but (according to the story) a certain Publius Clodius had disguised himself as a woman and gained admittance. The incident reminds us perhaps of student rag-week stunts; but it was used by Clodius' political opponents, mainly *optimates*, in an attempt to ruin his career. Cicero, who was still trying to keep on good terms with the *optimates*, spoke against Clodius, when the matter came to a trial. But Clodius had his supporters, and escaped, though undoubtedly guilty. His career survived, and he became very bitter against Cicero.

12. *A Roman Lady*

Cicero and Pompey draw closer together

At least, though, Cicero started to feel more confident about his friendship with Pompey. By the middle of 61, he could write to Atticus in these terms:

> 'The wretched poverty-stricken mobs, who suck the blood out of the public Treasury, think of me as the apple of Pompey's eye. Indeed, we have been joined in so many pleasing exchanges that the young aristocrats give him the nickname Gnaeus Cicero.' (*Gnaeus was Pompey's first name.*) [Cicero, *ad Att.* 1 16]

Allowing for some exaggeration, there must have been some grounds for

Cicero to feel that there was now a real chance of his working with Pompey in the way he had hinted when Pompey first returned from the East.

Problems with the *equites*

But problems for Cicero's plans started to arise from a different direction: compare the tone of the following letter with that written earlier in the year, when he was full of confidence in the Senate. Frequent shifts in mood like this were common in Cicero's letters. Perhaps they show that the whole idea of political harmony rested on very flimsy foundations, since a fairly small issue could change his tune so drastically:

'At Rome I find that politics are in a bit of a mess. Everything is unsatisfactory, and revolutions seem to be threatening. I am sure you've heard that our friends the *equites* are breaking away from the Senate. The first thing which upset them was a bill passed by the Senate about trying those who took bribes while serving on the jury in the courts. . . .

But there's another issue. It shows the *equites* to be acting with an almost incredible nerve, but I've done more than just put up with it— I've actually presented the case in as good a light as possible! It concerns the tax-companies (*publicani*) who won the right to collect taxes in Asia, after a fierce competition. They are now complaining that they paid too high a price for the contract, and have demanded that it should be cancelled. I was their foremost supporter—or should I say second, since Crassus was behind them in this demand. It's an appalling business, and their request is intolerable. But there was a great risk that if they didn't get their way, they would be completely torn apart from the Senate.' [Cicero, *ad Att.* 1 17]

This makes it clear that what was uppermost in the minds of the *equites* was not some splendid ideal of harmony with the Senate, but the thought of making sure that they did as well as possible financially. Cicero was obviously worried. In another letter to Atticus, written in January 60, his mood appears to have become still more gloomy:

'If I were to give you a brief summary of what has taken place since you left, you would be convinced that the State of Rome could not survive any longer. . . . Although the Senate had passed the bill about bribery on juries, no law has yet been carried. The Senate has been frightened off the law, and the *equites* have been offended. So a single year has overthrown the two pillars supporting the Republic, which were set up through my acts: the influence of the Senate has been lost, and the harmony of the orders has broken up.' [Cicero, *ad Att.* I 18]

Pompey's demands blocked

Early in this year, 60, Pompey was still frustrated by the *optimates* in his demands for land and the settlement of the Eastern wars. He turned to a tribune, called Flavius, who produced a bill aimed at getting land for Pompey's veterans. It was blocked by the Senate's use of another tribune's veto, and after a time Pompey and Flavius had to abandon the bill. Cicero had joined the opposition, although attempting to compromise. He was still planning to rely on Pompey to protect the State, and wrote to Atticus in March 60 in these terms:

> 'When, because of the acquittal of Clodius, I realised how corrupt the law-courts were, and when I found how easily the tax-collectors would split from the Senate, even if they had no quarrel with me, and finally since the rich (those friends of yours, the fish-fanciers) were openly jealous of me, I decided I must look around for greater support, and more dependable security. So I have brought Pompey, who at first had been silent about my achievements, to a position where he has stated often, and at length, that the safety of Rome and her Empire was due to me.' [Cicero, *ad Att.* I 19]

Pompey, so Cicero thought, would protect him from any hostility that might arise from other quarters. But Cicero was not being very realistic. If Pompey *had* been remaining on friendly terms with Cicero it was *not* because he was grateful to him for saving the State. Pompey wanted the support of the leading orator of the day in his attempts to pass the laws he needed. And this support was precisely what Cicero was refusing to give.

Caesar's stand for the consulship

So by now Pompey, despairing of ever getting anywhere with the Senate in the mood it was in, was starting to look around for fresh support. In the meantime, Cato's policy, of not giving in on the tax-contract, was winning the day, much to Cicero's annoyance. Cicero was still optimistic about Pompey, and even entertained hopes of winning over Julius Caesar to his side. Caesar had been in Spain as provincial governor, following his praetorship of 62, and would be standing for the consulship of 59. His impact on Roman politics had not so far been great, though he had played an important part in the events of the Catilinarian Conspiracy.

This is how Cicero, writing to Atticus, saw the situation in June 60:

> 'At the moment, since the *equites*, who once stood with me on the
> Capitoline Hill against the conspirators, with you as their standard-
> bearer and leader, have now abandoned the Senate, and since our
> highest-ranking citizens think themselves in Paradise if they can get
> bearded mullets to feed from their hand, surely I'm not doing so badly
> if I can gain the support of those who certainly could do the State
> serious harm if they had a mind to? (*It was Pompey and Caesar that he
> meant.*) As for our friend Cato, I am as fond of him as you are. But
> with the best possible intentions, and complete honesty, he sometimes
> harms the Republic. He talks as if he were living in the Ideal State of
> Plato, not the dunghill of Romulus. What could be fairer than for a
> man who takes bribes while on jury-service to be tried himself? This
> is what Cato wanted, and the Senate backed him. But the result was
> that the *equites* are quite at odds with the Senate—not with me, since I
> voted against the proposal.' [Cicero, *ad Att.* II 1]

In this letter, two things emerge clearly. One was that Cicero really
thought he had sufficient influence to keep Pompey and Caesar to the
course he wanted. Second, his view of politics was very much that it was
'the art of the possible'. There was no point in the sort of idealism that
Cato was showing. There were times when strict justice had to be sacrificed. It is not such an unusual opinion for a politician to hold—though
not all state that this is what they are doing quite so openly, and even
Cicero would hardly have made such an admission in a public statement.
Can we in fact be sure that Cato too did not have some reason for acting
as he did which went beyond the simple rights and wrongs of the case?
We are not in a position to examine *his* private thoughts.

The 'First Triumvirate'

There are no letters either from Cicero to Atticus for much of the year
60—a pity, because it was certainly in this period that events took a
dramatic turn, and one for which Cicero was apparently quite unprepared.
A later historian, Velleius, gives this account:

> A partnership of power was formed at this time between Caesar,
> Crassus and Pompey; its results were to bring ruin to the city, the
> world, and even, at different times, to each of the three men. Pompey
> joined the partnership because he hoped that Caesar would use his
> influence as consul to secure the settlement of his actions in the over-
> seas provinces, to which various people were still objecting. Caesar
> realised that by allowing Pompey this, his own influence would be

13. *Julius Caesar*

increased. Moreover, with Pompey carrying most of the unpopularity caused by the union, he would be in a stronger position. Crassus hoped that by using Pompey's prestige and Caesar's consular power, he would be able to reach a position which by himself he had failed to obtain. To strengthen the alliance, Caesar and Pompey arranged that Pompey should marry Julia, Caesar's daughter. [Velleius, II 44]

From this it can be seen that Caesar was in a strong bargaining position for the time being, since both Pompey and Crassus were being blocked by the Senate—Crassus being behind the *equites*' claim for a revision of the Asian tax-contract. Both Pompey's and Crassus' aims could be met by a strong consul—as Caesar certainly would be, if he could rely on the money, votes, and influence of the two most powerful men in Rome.

Should Cicero and the *optimates* have realised that this was the way events would turn? It is easy of course to look back and blame them for short-sighted attitudes. Cicero himself often spoke of the *optimates*, especially Cato, in these terms. But Cicero was a shrewd and intelligent politician, who had his ear close to the ground. The fact is that even he was taken by surprise, and from this we must conclude that the move was unpredictable. The long-standing differences of opinion between Pompey and Crassus must have been so well known that it was not believed they could patch them up in order to work with Caesar. And of course the partnership was far from secure at any time. Historians have long given the title 'the First Triumvirate' to the grouping, but apart from the fact that a 'Triumvirate' was strictly speaking a legally established body, the term suggests a much closer and more stable relationship than actually was the case.

Cicero's attitude to the Triumvirate

By December 60, Cicero certainly had some idea what was going on, since Caesar had been making efforts to win him over. Cicero was tempted:

> 'In favour of this course, there are the following advantages: a very close connexion with Pompey, and Caesar too, if I should want it; I shall be reunited with my enemies, and will win peace with regard to the common people; and I shall have a quiet old age.' [Cicero, *ad Att.* II 3]

But he resisted the temptation: he saw the partnership as opposed to all he had stood for as consul. Caesar however had wanted Cicero's support, and continued to try for it. We should not forget how much damage or good Cicero's brilliance as a speaker could do to a cause. Moreover Caesar always had a very high regard for Cicero, which was to some extent returned by the latter—both were men with a deep respect for literary excellence, and each acknowledged the other as a leader in this field. Cicero, therefore, in refusing to join Caesar put his ideal—the *Respublica* which he knew and loved—before a safe course which he could not believe in.

59: Caesar's consulship

The year 59, the consulship of Caesar and Bibulus, was in every way an eventful one—eventful for both the consuls, for Cicero, and indeed for everyone in the political set-up. Bibulus was a strong supporter of the *optimates*, and firmly opposed to Caesar. Caesar in his turn made it clear that he would not be stopped by Bibulus, despite the backing his fellow-consul had from such men as Cato. At last land was found for Pompey's veterans, and the Eastern settlement was agreed. In addition the tax-collectors in Asia received the revision of the contract, which they had long been seeking. One measure adopted by the Senate to stop Caesar becoming too powerful had been a proposal that after his consulship his province should be the supervision of the 'woods and paths' of Italy. This would have been an empty task, with none of the lure of the big overseas province. Caesar was not going to put up with this, and used the by now familiar device of employing a tribune to pass a law in the Assembly. This law, passed by Vatinius, gave him the province of Cisalpine Gaul and Illyricum (see map of Roman Empire on p. 75). Later Transalpine Gaul was added to this.

From Cicero's letters we can get some idea of how Rome reacted to these moves. Pompey, although definitely behind the measures of Caesar, was trying not to appear too committed. In April 59, Cicero expressed it like this:

> 'Pompey has fenced so far with the important questions. When asked, he said that he agreed with Caesar's laws. But what about his methods? "Caesar must answer that for himself," he replied.' [Cicero, *ad Att.* II 16]

The attempts to oppose Caesar

Caesar's land bill and the rest of his programme, including some social reforms, were now bound to succeed. It was a very different situation from 63, when Catiline had been driven to extreme methods by a lack of political power. Now not only was Caesar consul, but there was Pompey's great influence as well. Plutarch records that shortly after Pompey's public replies to the questions about Caesar's laws, Pompey flooded Rome with his soldiers and controlled everything by force. Even if this is not strictly true, force was a very strong factor. Caesar's opponents could not risk open violence. Although they knew that Caesar's laws were technically invalid, this counted for nothing at the time. There were in fact two reasons why Caesar's measures were illegal, the first being that they were carried *per vim*—by means of force—and the second that Bibulus had resorted to an unusual, but perhaps constitutionally correct method of blocking them. We can learn what happened to Bibulus:

> Finally, when Bibulus saw no other way of stopping the bill going through, he proclaimed that all the remaining days of the year were to be regarded as a 'sacred period'. This meant that it was legally impossible for the people even to meet in an assembly. But Caesar paid little attention to this, and fixed his day for the passing of the land law. [Dio, xxxviii 6]

This was not all that Bibulus suffered, as Plutarch makes clear:

> His lictors (*the official bodyguards of the consul*) had their *fasces* (*the rods which were the symbol of power*) broken, two of the tribunes who were with him were wounded, and he himself had a bucket of manure thrown over his head. [Plutarch, *Life of Pompey* 48]

Clodius and the tribunate

At this stage Cicero was in such a state that he went so far as to say that Clodius was the only hope. Clodius, since his trial for the *Bona Dea* scandal, had been working closely with Crassus, and so was bound to follow the wishes of Caesar and Pompey to some extent. The year 59 was important for him too, since he was hoping to stand for the position of tribune for 58. This was complicated by the fact that he was not a plebeian, but a patrician. The office of tribune, since it had been set up to protect the interests of the plebeians, was not open to patricians—although it was possible to be adopted into the plebeians. (The closest modern equivalent is the case of a member of the House of Lords who wishes to be made a 'commoner' in order to make a political career in the House of Commons.) For a while, Cicero was very indignant that some of the Senate were trying to stop Clodius becoming a plebeian. If he had known what Clodius' tribunate would bring for him, he would have been less annoyed at them. In any case, with the backing of Caesar and Crassus, Clodius *was* registered as a plebeian, and elected tribune for the following year.

Clodius' threats

By July 59 Cicero had changed his tune about Clodius. Clodius had started to issue threats that he would prosecute Cicero for putting the Catilinarians to death without a trial. Cicero wrote a succession of tortured letters to Atticus which show the state of his mind. The most revealing is the following:

> 'There are many things which worry me—both because of the unsettled state of politics, and because of threats to my personal safety. . . . The threatenings of Clodius, and the prospect of a fight, only worry me slightly. I can either face the music with complete dignity, I imagine, or lean out of the way without any trouble. I can hear you saying, "Enough of that old-fashioned dignity: safety's what matters now". Oh dear, I wish you were with me. You wouldn't be at a loss. Perhaps I am rather blinded, too much in love with my ideals. I can assure you, there was never a situation so shameful, offensive and dreadful to every kind of man as the present state of affairs. . . .

> Bibulus is praised sky-high—I don't know why; he's treated as another Fabius Maximus, as though like him he was saving the State by his delaying tactics. I'm afraid that Pompey, my former friend, has ruined his good reputation. It hurts me to say it. The three of them are liked by no one; I'm afraid they'll only get their way by the use of terror. I don't express opposition to their cause, because I can't forget my friendship for Pompey, but to approve would be to make my own career look like nonsense. Popular opinion is shown in the theatre and shows. At the gladiator games, both Pompey himself and his supporters were showered with hisses, and at the games of Apollo, an actor, Diphilus, got in an attack on Pompey the Great: "You have become Great—by ruining us." He had to repeat the line a thousand times. . . . When Caesar entered, the applause died down completely. . . .

> What's more, there *are* those threats of Clodius against me. He's definitely an enemy, and there's trouble in store of such a kind that I only hope you can come at once. I think I can still rely on the support of all the loyal citizens, and even those who are fairly loyal— the ones who were on my side when I was consul, that is. Pompey is going out of his way to show goodwill to me. He asserts that Clodius won't lift a finger against me. He may believe that himself, but he doesn't fool me. . . .

> Caesar wishes me to accept a post of responsibility under him. This would be quite a good way out of the danger. But I don't *want* to get out of it. Why's that? I'd rather fight. But really I can't decide. If only you were here! Well, if it's really vital, I'll call you. What else can I say? All I can think is that everything is lost—why beat about the bush?' [Cicero *ad Att.* ii 19]

The letters to Atticus continued thick and fast, the tone similar in many of them, since Cicero was gradually becoming more and more aware of the reality of the danger from Clodius. At one stage he was hopeful that the Triumvirate would break up, and there were some grounds for thinking it might. Leaving aside the unpopularity Cicero describes above, one factor was that once Pompey had gained what he needed from Caesar, he might always try to go back to supporting the Senate. So Caesar had to work hard to keep Pompey with him, and for this reason he was worried about Cicero. If there was anyone with the persuasiveness to turn Pompey away from Caesar and Crassus, it was Cicero. So Caesar made repeated offers to him, hoping he would join the partnership. But Cicero continued to refuse, despite the doubts expressed above, and later in 59 Caesar must have decided to support Clodius' plan to get rid of Cicero. Although in the late summer there was a rather mysterious plot (which might have destroyed the partnership if it had succeeded), at the end of the year the Triumvirate was still intact. We can let Suetonius, in his life of Caesar, have the last word on 59:

> Later on, Caesar controlled all the affairs of State just as he wished. People who had to sign public papers started to make jokes to the effect that the business had not been conducted during the consulship of Caesar and Bibulus, but that of Julius and Caesar. There was a verse current at the time which went as follows:
>> The consulship of Caesar was a most eventful year,
>> But the consulship of Bibulus was *very* dull, I fear!
> [Suetonius, *Div. Jul.* 20]

5

From Exile to Civil War

Clodius' bill against Cicero

The story of the opening months of 58, Clodius' tribunate, can be told quickly, in the words of Velleius (a man with an obvious bias):

> Publius Clodius was engaged in a bitter campaign against Cicero, full of hatred—how could there be any love between two people so different? After being transferred to the plebeians from the patricians, he became tribune, and during his year of office introduced a bill which said that 'Anyone who had executed a Roman citizen without trial should be forbidden fire and water'. (*The Roman phrase meaning that a person should be made an exile*.) Cicero was not mentioned by name in the law, but he was the target, and he alone. So this man who had given so much service to his State was outlawed, a tragedy and a poor reward for saving his country. There was more than a hint that Caesar and Pompey were behind it. [Velleius, II 45]

Plutarch gives a vivid description of Cicero's reactions to the threat of exile:

> Finding that he was in danger of being prosecuted, Cicero put on mourning-clothes, and with his hair worn long and straggly, walked round the city, appealing to the people for help. But he could not enter a single street without being met by Clodius and a band of insolent thugs, who interrupted his appeals by passing all kinds of rude jokes about the change in his clothing-style, and his manner of conducting himself; often they threw mud and stones at him. In spite of this, almost all the *equites* changed into mourning to show their sympathy, and he was accompanied in his appeals by at least 20,000 young men, their hair uncut like his own. [Plutarch, *Life of Cicero* 30]

But it was to no avail. Plutarch describes how as a last attempt Cicero went up to Pompey's house in the country—Pompey had chosen to be out of Rome while this was going on:

However, Pompey could not face the thought of seeing him. He was deeply ashamed, thinking of all the times when Cicero had taken his side in politics. But Pompey was now Caesar's son-in-law, and since Caesar asked him to, he betrayed his former loyalties. By slipping out of the back door of the house, he avoided seeing Cicero. [Plutarch, *Life of Cicero* 31]

It should be clear that the matter was not quite as straightforward as Plutarch would have us believe. We have seen that in the past decade Cicero *had* often sided with Pompey—but there had also been times when he had let him down. It may be that Pompey would have agreed that Cicero needed to be taught that his opposition was not going to be tolerated.

Cicero in exile

When we look at the letters Cicero wrote while in exile, we see a new side of his character, and it is not particularly attractive. From the moment he left Rome, on 20 March 58 or thereabouts, he was shattered. At first he stayed in the area of Rome, but Clodius, now sure of success, passed a second bill which exiled Cicero by name and also (a matter which caused him bitterness and constant trouble) ordered his property to be confiscated. The map shows his route into exile. He was forced to leave Italy, and spent much of his time writing to his family and friends.

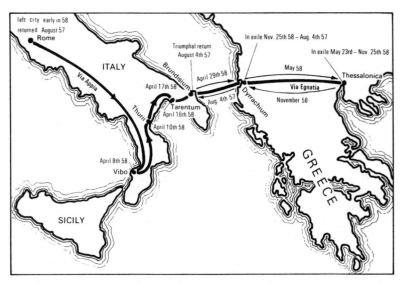

14. *Cicero's route into exile* (*April 58–August 57* BC)

D

15. *A Roman married couple*

Nothing has yet been said about Cicero's family. He had married, in about 80, a well-to-do woman called Terentia. Up to the time of his exile, he seems to have lived happily enough with her. The older of the two children was a daughter, Tullia, who was greatly loved by Cicero (he calls her Tulliola, a pet-name). The younger was a boy, Marcus, born in 65. The following extract comes from a letter he wrote to them just before leaving Italy:

To Terentia, Tulliola, and   Brundisium,
young Marcus Cicero (at Rome)   29 April, 58

If I write to you less often than I might, it is because, apart from the fact that my whole life is utterly miserable, whenever I start to write to you or to read one of your letters, I break down in tears, and can't bear it. If only I had clung less to life! In that case I should have had very little to be sorry about in my lifetime. . . .

I am setting out from Brundisium, and making for Cyzicus, via Macedonia. How hopeless, how wretched it all is! What can I do? Can I ask you to come, Terentia, when you are unwell both in body and mind? But what if I don't ask you—must I be separated from you? What it amounts to is this: if there is any hope of my return, please stay and help push it forward; but if, as I am afraid, all is finished, make your way to me however you can. Please bear in mind that while I have you, I shall not feel that I am completely lost. But what will become of my dear Tulliola? You must see to that now—I can't think of a thing. I know that, whatever our situation, we must do all we can to give the poor girl a happy marriage and a good name. And what about my son, young Cicero? I wish I could always hold him on my knee and in my arms! I can't carry on writing, I'm so upset. I don't know whether you have anything at all left, or have been completely plundered, as I fear may have happened. . . .

Look after yourself as well as you possibly can, and remember that I am more affected by your distress than my own. Goodbye, dear Terentia, my good and loyal wife; goodbye, my dearest little daughter, and you, Cicero, the last hope of our family. [Cicero, ad Fam. xiv 4]

This shows Cicero as a man with very strong feelings for his family—a side of a Roman politician which is very rarely seen. But it does seem rather a violent outburst. It is hard to bear such floods of weeping and self-pity (despite what Cicero says about being more concerned about his family's misfortunes than his own), but we should not forget how severe the shock of exile was. Very few men of public note were exiled from Rome during this period, and certainly not many who thought of themselves as the saviour of their State. Also, the 'British' way of bearing misfortunes—the 'stiff upper lip', and hiding of all sign of emotion—is not, perhaps, the natural way for Italians to react: Cicero shows here that he possesses the violent emotions that we often describe as belonging to the 'Latin temperament'. But even if we can understand why he took exile so badly, it would still have to be admitted that at times his tone, as a recent writer on Cicero has put it, 'reminds one of a petulant and emotionally self-indulgent child. Some of the letters can only be described as "whining".' For example, the following one to his brother:

'Please don't blame me, my dear Quintus, for ruining you and the whole family by this terrible tragedy of mine. I haven't acted wrongly or dishonestly—it was just that I was short-sighted and in such a miserable state. I didn't do *anything* you could call wicked—all I did was trust people who I thought should never have deceived me, because of their close and sacred connexions with me. . . . It was only the tears of my friends which stopped me taking the escape-route of death. To die would certainly have been the best thing for me, the best way out of my sorrows, which are too heavy to be endured.' [Cicero, ad *Quintum fratrem* i 4]

The move to recall Cicero

There was much more in this style. For the rest of the year 58 and the first half of 57, Cicero was in constant doubt whether he would ever be recalled. Friends had in fact been working very hard to reverse Clodius' law, and rumours about the likelihood of being able to return must have kept coming to Cicero, who cannot have known whether to believe them or not. By November 58 he had become quite hopeful, and returned to Dyrrachium, the nearest town to Italy on the other side of the Adriatic. Then one of the consuls for 57, Lentulus, moved a bill in the Senate proposing Cicero's recall. But Clodius was not finished yet, and with the help of two of the tribunes blocked the move. A very sinister development was the increasing use by Clodius of armed gangs—Cicero's brother Quintus was almost killed, and he himself, still nervously waiting in Dyrrachium, was thrown again into gloom. For the next six months, Cicero's friends worked hard, none harder than Pompey. No doubt he felt that Cicero had suffered enough, and would now stop opposing him. Pompey argued that Cicero had indeed saved his country, and soon the Senate passed a motion ruling that anyone who tried to prevent Cicero's recall would be regarded as a public enemy. Clodius' gang warfare tactics were also challenged. Two of Cicero's supporters, Sestius and Milo, trained gangs of their own. Milo got a squad of gladiators for the purpose. This street fighting was to be a common sight in Rome for the next five years.

16. *A gladiator (retiarius or net-fighter)*

Cicero's return

Eventually the bill was passed. Clodius could resist no longer. Perhaps the severity and brutality of his revenge against Cicero lost him much of his support—he burned Cicero's country villas, and looted them with his gangs. He completely destroyed Cicero's town house in Rome, and built a temple to Liberty on the site. Plutarch says that 'all this was so shameful that it made Pompey bitterly sorry about the way he had deserted Cicero'.

Cicero, not surprisingly, was overjoyed at the news, and the reception he got on reaching Italy must have been quite overwhelming. This is how he described the events to Atticus:

'On 4 August I started out from **Dyrrachium**—that was the day the law about me was carried. I arrived at Brundisium on the next day, where I was met by my dear Tulliola. It was her birthday, and also the anniversary of the founding of the colony of Brundisium, and the Temple of **Prosperity**, which is near your house. The crowds there noticed the coincidence, and celebrated enthusiastically, congratulating me warmly. On the 8th, I heard from Quintus (I was still at Brundisium) that the Assembly had passed the bill. . . . By the time I approached Rome, just about everyone, of every possible rank, who was known to my slave (*this was a slave with the duty of reminding Cicero of the names of all the people he might meet*) came towards me. The only ones who weren't there were private enemies who couldn't hide or deny the fact that they were my enemies. When I reached the Capena Gate of the city, the steps of the temples were crowded with people from the lower classes, who cheered me thunderously. This kind of applause, and huge crowds, escorted me all the way up to the Capitoline Hill.' [Cicero, *ad Att.* IV I]

Problems in Rome

Cicero was again filled with confidence. Pompey seemed prepared to work closely with him, and Cicero realised how much he owed to Pompey. However, his first involvement in politics brought him straight to another tricky problem. Pompey was after a new command—the control of the Roman corn-supplies. There was a serious food-shortage in Rome, and Cicero proposed that a special commission should be given to Pompey. So far, so good. But Cicero discovered that the Senate was very cool about the idea of handing over such powers to Pompey. Also, a tribune, called Messius, proposed another bill giving Pompey far greater powers than those suggested in Cicero's bill. As on many other occasions, Pompey's own attitude was the difficult thing. Cicero wrote to Atticus on the subject:

'My bill, which the consuls have put forward, is quite a reasonable proposal: that of Messius is just too much. Pompey *says* he's in favour of mine, but his friends say he really prefers the other. . . . I am keeping quiet, therefore—especially since I don't yet know what is to happen to my house.' [*Ibid.*]

This was another thing which made Cicero rather cautious. He was claiming compensation for the destruction of his property by Clodius. He would not feel happy until this was settled. It *was* settled, and fairly soon. Clodius' temple to Liberty was to be pulled down. Cicero was satisfied with the arrangements with regard to his town house, not with

17. *The hall in a town house*

those for the villas which had been ruined. But in any case the battle with Clodius was not yet quite over, as this letter, written in November 57, shows:

'On 3 November, the workmen were driven off the building site for my new house by armed gangsters. The porch which was being repaired had nearly got as far as the roof, but then it was knocked down again. My brother Quintus' house (*next door to Cicero's*) was first smashed up by stones hurled from my site, and then set on fire by Clodius' orders. The whole city watched as firebrands were thrown in, with loud cries of horror—not just from loyal citizens (I don't think they exist any longer), but from the people in general. Clodius is a madman running riot. His next scheme will be nothing less than the murder of his enemies.' [Cicero, *ad Att.* IV 3]

Clodius and Milo

Another political issue was in hot debate in Rome at the time. The details need not be discussed here, but it involved a command in Egypt which would bring considerable power and prestige to anyone who secured it. Both Pompey and Crassus were interested, and so was Lentulus, the consul in 57 who had proposed Cicero's recall. This put Cicero in a difficult position. Clodius was not slow to exploit the situation, on behalf of *his* backer Crassus. He had been appointed aedile for 56, thus avoiding trial on a charge of violence. The charge had been brought by Milo; Clodius hit back by prosecuting Milo himself for the same offence. In February 56, Cicero wrote to his brother:

'On 2 February, Milo appeared for trial, with Pompey in support . . . we came off rather well, and the case was adjourned till the 7th. . . . On the 7th, Milo duly appeared. Pompey spoke, or rather tried to speak. For as soon as he rose to his feet, Clodius' thugs raised an uproar, so that throughout his speech there were interruptions—not just hostile shouts, but downright abuse and insults. But Pompey was not put off, and with great courage finished his speech, saying all that he intended to say. He even had the authority to get silence for his words at times. After he had finished, Clodius stood up to reply. Our side then greeted him with such a shout (they were determined to get their own back) that he completely caved in, losing control of his voice, expression and mind. This went on from about 11 a.m., when Pompey finished, till 1 p.m. Clodius was really angry—white with rage!—and kept asking questions to his followers, shouting above the din: "Who has been starving the poor?" "Pompey!" replied the gang. "Who wants to go to Egypt?" "Pompey!" "Who do *you* want to go?" "Crassus!" (Crassus was there at the time, and not exactly friendly towards Milo.) About an hour later, as though at a signal, the supporters of Clodius started spitting at our men. Anger burst out. Clodius' lot started trying to push us back, and so our side went for them. The gang fled. Clodius was thrown from the platform, and I made my escape, for fear of getting hurt in the riots.' [Cicero, *ad Q. fr.* II 2]

An awkward situation, in more ways than one. Scenes like this were becoming more frequent all the time. As far as the Egyptian question was concerned, Cicero was still unsure—particularly as Pompey was not making it any clearer what he really wanted.

Problems for the Triumvirate

Early in 56, it must have been obvious that not all was well for the Triumvirate. Pompey and Crassus were openly quarrelling, and the gang-warfare between Milo and Clodius highlighted this. Cicero again started to be sure that the trio were bound to break up, and his political activities showed what he meant to do about it. The hope was that Pompey could be persuaded to leave Caesar's side (as Cicero had hoped before his exile, too) and go over to the Senate and *optimates*, to protect the Republic from the dangerous *populares*. So Cicero attacked one of Caesar's bills in the Senate, in his attempt to force the breach between Caesar and Pompey. Unfortunately for Cicero, the effect of his action was very different.

Conference at Luca

At this time there was talk in the Senate about the possibility of recalling Caesar from Gaul. Crassus, unhappy about the way things were going for the Triumvirate, went to see Caesar at Ravenna, and the two of them arranged to meet Pompey at Luca (Northern Italy), in April 56. One hundred and twenty senators who supported them were also there. The result of the meeting was that the differences were patched up. Some bargaining went on that gave all three partners considerably more power. The first step was that Pompey and Crassus were to be consuls for 55. This had a double effect. For a start, it made sure that none of Caesar's opponents could get in. For a second thing, it would give the other two members the opportunity to have military commands at the end of their year. In return for this, Caesar had his command in Gaul renewed for a further five years.

56 after consol alloed to so out to he country.

Cicero's position after Luca

Apart from the new powers which all three had decided on, the most important single result concerned Cicero. For all his brave show of resisting the partnership, he was quickly and effectively told to stop opposing their acts—even if he did not feel he could actively support them. His political career from now on showed a dramatic reversal. It was, in fact, the end of his importance as a political force—at least until the final months of his life. He appears to have felt that the Senatorial party had failed once again, by giving in to the demands of Caesar, Pompey and Crassus, and he wrote something—possibly a public letter—in which he outlined his new position, one of support for all that Pompey and even the other two might do. He wrote to Atticus explaining his action, and referring to his 'palinode' (a withdrawal of his previous views, and statement of his new ones):

> 'I suppose my "palinode" *was* rather shameful. But goodbye to honesty, truth and honour in politics! . . . Since those who have no political power do not wish to be my friends, I shall make sure that I win the affection of those who *are* in power. I can hear you say, "I wish you'd decided that a long time ago!" Well, I know that's what you wanted, and I admit I've been an absolute ass.' [Cicero, *ad Att.* IV 5]

The frustration of his situation

So over the next five years, Cicero remained on the sidelines. He gave a much greater part of his time to various literary activities—including some attempts at poetry which were notoriously bad. But at the same time he did produce some major works on oratory and on the State. His public life was more or less confined to the law-courts, and here too he was far from being a free agent. The worst aspect of his political position was that he had to defend friends of Caesar and Crassus who had previously been bitter enemies of his. This was bound to place a strain on a man who for a time had been so close to the centre of political affairs—and at times this broke through in his letters to Atticus:

> 'Really, what could be more humiliating than the present situation, especially for me? I know you too are naturally interested in politics, but you aren't bound to be anyone's slave in particular—you're in the same boat as everybody. But for me, just think what I must feel! If I give my true opinion on politics I am considered mad; if I say what commonsense suggests I *must* say, then I am a slave; if I say nothing, I am a helpless captive.' [Cicero, *ad Att.* IV 6]

The same mood comes over in a letter to Quintus, written late in 54: he is explaining the stage his intended poem about Caesar's expedition to Britain in 54 had reached:

> I would do the poem as well as I could, but you will understand that if one is to write poetry, one's mind must be alive. In the present times, mine cannot be. Granted that by taking myself away from political concerns I can devote myself to literary work; but still, I can tell you something I would rather have hidden in the past—from you especially. Quintus, my dear brother, it breaks my heart to think that there is no longer a Republic, no courts of justice, and that I must pass those years during which I should have been full of dignity and prestige in the Senate, by working on lawsuits and studying at home, so as to make life tolerable. The dream I once had of surpassing the rest of mankind—it's gone completely. I have left off attacking my enemies—I have even defended some.' [Cicero, ad Q. fr. III 5]

But for the most part, Cicero was less pessimistic than this. At about the same time he wrote to Atticus:

> 'You wonder how I'm taking all this. Quite calmly, actually—and very proud of myself I am too for doing so. We have lost not only the essential ingredients of a free State; even the outward appearance of freedom, which it used to have, has gone. There is no Republic left to cheer and console me. And can I take *that* in my stride? Why, yes. I have the memory of the splendid show the Republic once put on, when I was in command—and the gratitude I received in return. . . . And I turn back to the kind of life I most enjoy, books and studying. The hard work of conducting defences is balanced by the pleasure which oratory gives me. I am delighted with my town house and country villas. What I remember is not the great height from which I have fallen, but the depth from which I have emerged. If I can have your company and that of my brother, *they* can go and hang themselves for all I care.' [Cicero, ad Att. IV 18]

Crassus' and Pompey's consulship

After Luca, Pompey and Crassus, because of their consulship for 55, obtained military commands which would put them on Caesar's level. Caesar therefore had to do some hard thinking, in order to keep his own cause strong in Rome. He risked finding himself in a position similar to that of Pompey in Asia, of returning to find his position much weaker. It was probably with this in mind that Caesar planned the invasion of Britain. If so, it was not very successful.

18. *Julius Caesar*

The year 55 itself passed quite uneventfully. Pompey and Crassus were mainly concerned with their provinces—Crassus with Syria, Pompey with Spain. At the end of 55, Crassus set off for the East. Pompey, however, stayed in Italy, and this gave him the political initiative. He was there in theory to look after the corn-supply; and while he was not allowed into the city of Rome, because of his command of Spain, he could keep troops under arms, in or around the city. He could always say they were on their way to Spain, where lieutenants were looking after affairs.

The collapse of the Triumvirate

The year 54 was a difficult year for Caesar in Gaul, with the second invasion of Britain failing to achieve all he wished. Things were made worse in the autumn by the death of his daughter Julia, who was married to Pompey.

No doubt Caesar and Pompey were genuinely upset—Pompey and Julia apparently got on very well. Caesar in particular, though, could hardly have failed to think about the political side of her death. It was now clearer than ever that the 'friendship' with Pompey was based on rather insecure foundations. There was also the absence of Crassus, and the lack of anyone apart from Pompey who could have controlled affairs in the city, which was constantly troubled by violence and bribery.

Caesar therefore relied heavily on agents supporting his cause in Rome. Quintus Cicero was on his staff, and Caesar was anxious to keep on good terms with the elder Cicero. Cicero was delighted with his present popularity with Caesar, as was shown in his letters, especially to Quintus:

> 'I am really pleased to learn from your letters about Caesar's affection for me. But I'm not depending too much on the offers he makes: I'm not interested in public offices, and have no taste for glory. I am more concerned to make sure of his goodwill than with his promises.' [Cicero, *ad Q. fr.* III 6]

In the autumn of the year 53, the news reached Rome that Crassus, together with his army, had been destroyed in a battle against the Parthians at Carrhae. It was a crushing defeat, the worst suffered by the Romans for many years. The poet Ovid later summed up the disgrace in a few words:

> On the Euphrates, Crassus lost his standards, his son, his men, and in the end his life. [Ovid, *Fasti* VI 397]

The Triumvirate was now reduced to two men, whose interests seemed to be fast drawing further and further apart.

52: Clodius and Milo

In Rome during that year unrest and trouble had continued, and in January 52 the trouble reached a head. After the unsuccessful attempt of Clodius to prosecute Milo in 56, there had been frequent outbursts of gang warfare over the next few years. The new year (52) began without the appointment of any consuls. Milo was a candidate for the consulship. He was strongly supported by the *optimates*, and there is reason to think that his earlier friendship with Pompey had grown rather cold—indeed, that Pompey may have regarded him as a threat to his own supremacy at Rome. Cicero reported the events as follows:

'Clodius realised that Milo would be elected consul, backed by all the Roman people. He was therefore worried that this would restrict his own power, since he was to be praetor. So he offered his help to the other candidates.... He started working furiously, but the greater his efforts, the more Milo's support grew. When Clodius, a man who would stop at nothing, realised that his bitterest enemy was after all certainly going to be made consul, and saw that the Roman people weren't just saying that they approved of him, but were actually going to vote for him, he started to come out into the open with his plans, and say in public that Milo ought to be killed.' [Cicero, *pro Milone* 25]

But Milo wasn't killed, and Clodius was. What happened was this:

(*On* 18 *January*) 'Milo ran into Clodius in front of his estate. It was about 5 o'clock. He was at once set upon from higher ground. After his coachman was stopped and killed, Milo threw away his cloak, jumped from the carriage and defended himself determinedly. Some of Clodius' men ran to the carriage, their swords drawn, in order to attack Milo from behind. Others, who thought he had already been killed, started hacking down the slaves who escorted him. Some of the slaves, who were fighting round the carriage, tried to go to help him. They could not do so, and when they heard from Clodius' mouth that Milo was dead, they believed it. So these slaves, without orders, and without their master there or knowing about it, did just

19. *A two-horse carriage*

what anyone would have hoped his slaves would do in such a situation. Please note that I am not trying to take the blame from Milo, just to record the facts.' [Cicero, *pro Milone* 27]

Despite what Cicero says, this is bound to be a biased account, since it comes from the speech he planned to give when Milo was subsequently put on trial. For the events of the trial itself, we have this account:

> Among those convicted were Milo and others, charged with killing Clodius. Milo was being defended by Cicero, but when he reached the court, and saw Pompey and a vast array of soldiers, he was unable to give a word of his prepared speech. He just got out a few stumbling words, which faded on his lips, and then sat down with great relief. [Dio, XL 54]

In the event, the jury decided that the first wounding of Clodius happened without Milo's knowledge, but that after he was wounded he was put to death on Milo's orders. So Milo was banished, and went into exile at Massilia (Marseilles). When he was there he received a copy of the speech that Cicero intended to deliver. 'Just as well', he said, 'that the court didn't get a chance to hear it. Otherwise I would never have been able to enjoy the splendid sea-food of Marseilles.'

Pompey's sole consulship

The killing of Clodius emphasised that Rome needed strong control, if the rule of law was to have any chance of surviving. As there were still no officials in Rome, more people than ever were talking about the need for a *dictator*. Cato and his followers were afraid that the situation would be taken out of their hands by force. Rather than allow a dictatorship, the *optimates* decided to propose that Pompey be made sole consul for 52. To this the Senate agreed.

The fear of another *dictator* was obviously a strong one. If we recall the events of Sulla's dictatorship, it is easy enough to understand. Even if Pompey was effectively doing the same job, it did at least appear that he was rather more limited in his powers, and he acted in a way which did something to soothe the fears of another Sulla.

Pompey passed a lot of legislation, some obviously designed to please the Senate, some more favourable to Caesar. Pompey had not yet committed himself to a definite split from Caesar, although he wanted to make sure Caesar's position was an uncomfortable one. Caesar had enough troubles of his own in Gaul, without worrying about what Pompey was up to in Italy:

The news of Pompey's actions reached Gaul quickly. The Gauls added to the rumours, putting in extra details which sounded quite convincing—that Caesar was kept away from his army because of the troubles in the city. These developments helped trigger off the rebellion of those who were becoming more bitter about being under Roman rule. They started planning more openly and more daringly. [Caesar, *de Bello Gallico* VII 1]

The rebellion which began was a very serious one. Led by a young chieftain called Vercingetorix, it brought in almost all the Gallic tribes against Rome. After a hard struggle, the campaign was successfully completed by Caesar by the end of the year. But Caesar knew that both Pompey and the *optimates* were gaining in strength in relation to his own position.

One other event of the year 52 was a law which stated that there must be a five-year gap between holding office as consul or praetor, and taking up a provincial command as proconsul or propraetor. An immediate effect was that Cicero was summoned to take command of the province of Cilicia (see map of Roman Empire). Despite his determination to stay in Rome, he now had to leave, and at a critical moment.

Cicero's provincial command

Cicero was to be out of Rome for eighteen months. The wealth of correspondence from Cilicia tells us a lot about Cicero, and a lot about

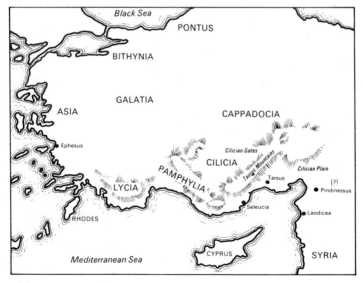

20. *Cilicia and Asia Minor*

provincial government. Cicero was inheriting the province from a man who had been a mixture of incompetence and intolerance, and who had succeeded only in annoying everyone in the province. Like many other governors, Cicero's predecessor had regarded the provinces first and foremost as a way of feathering his own nest. Although in recent years, thanks to Caesar, some efforts had been made to tighten control of the actions of governors, there was still endless scope for making a pile—by legitimate expenses and takings from wars. Cicero was horrified with the situation, and complained bitterly to Atticus about the mess that Cilicia was in. He himself had certain ideals—the man who had prosecuted Verres, nearly twenty years before, was determined to act in a humane and generous way towards those among whom he worked. Yet, for all this, it was clear right from the start, that his heart was not in the province:

To Atticus   Athens, 29 June 51

'I reached Athens on 25 June, and I've been waiting three days now for my Chief of Staff, Pomptinus. There's no definite information about when he'll arrive. . . . So far we have caused absolutely no expense, either publicly or privately. We haven't even taken the amount allowed to us under Caesar's law, or made any demands upon the people who have looked after us. The whole staff are making sure my good reputation does not suffer. So far, so good. The Greeks have noticed this, and are talking about it with pleasure. In other things too I am taking great care, as you wished. But we won't expect applause until the final curtain.
The general situation makes me keep blaming myself for not getting out of the business. It's just not me! "Let the shoemaker stick to his last", as the saying goes. "What, already?", you will say. "But you haven't even *got* to the business yet." I know *that* all right—the worst is still ahead. I think I'm putting up a pretty good show, but deep down within me, I'm hating it.' [Cicero, *ad Att.* v 10]

Caelius

Before leaving, Cicero had taken great trouble to find someone who could be relied on to know the ins and outs of the complicated political developments at Rome, and who would be sure to keep him well-informed. The person he chose was a young man called Caelius. Cicero had previously defended him successfully, and knew that he was well in with everybody who mattered. So, fortunately, the absence of Cicero from Rome does not deprive us of our first-hand evidence for what was going on—since Caelius saw all that would have been seen by Cicero, and, because of Cicero's distance from Rome, had to go into even more detail than Cicero would have had to when writing to Atticus. This is the start of the first letter Caelius sent to Cicero after his departure for Cilicia:

> 'On the subject of the promise I made to you when you left me, namely that I would give you a really careful account of what goes on in Rome, I have got hold of a man who is prepared to go into every detail. He's so thorough, you might find what he says too long-winded! But I know how eager you are to find out everything. . . .
>
> If you bumped into Pompey, as you hoped to, let me know what you thought of him, what he said to you, and which way he's thinking of turning. (He's in the habit of saying one thing while thinking another; but he can't hide what he really thinks—he's not clever enough!) There are some pretty nasty rumours flying about concerning Caesar, but it's only hearsay . . . there's no definite news yet. Even the rumours aren't generally known, though they're an open enough secret in the sort of circles you move in. . . . You yourself died on 24 May—according to the idlers outside the courts, that is! (I wish *they* were dead!) The rumour was all over the Forum and the city that you had been murdered on the road.' [Cicero, *ad Fam.* VIII 1]

Events at Rome

At Rome, the year 51 saw the *optimates* strengthening their ranks against Caesar. After the crushing of Vercingetorix' revolt, Caesar's work in Gaul could be said to be virtually over. This meant that the pressure to get Caesar recalled, which had started five years earlier (before the Conference of Luca prolonged his command) became much fiercer. One of the consuls, Marcus Marcellus, was in the forefront of the opposition to Caesar. The following event took place early in 51:

> The consul Marcus Claudius Marcellus, after announcing in public that he had an important proposal to make, brought to the Senate a motion that Caesar should be replaced in Gaul before the time-limit. The reason for this, he argued, was that since the war was over and peace had been declared, the winning army ought to be disbanded. He added that Caesar should not be allowed to stand for the consulship in absence. [Suetonius, *Div. Jul.* 28]

What exactly was going on here? The main strength of the *optimates'* position was that if Caesar returned home as a *private* citizen, he could be tried for passing laws by means of violence during his consulship of 59. (*Public* officials could not be prosecuted, and this included proconsuls as well as consuls.) Because of this, Caesar was planning to be elected as

E

21. *Legionaries building a camp*

consul for the year 48 (the first legal date for re-election), while still in
Gaul. If he could do this he could return to Rome as consul, then leave
again as proconsul, and escape trial. Naturally enough, the *optimates* were
determined not to allow Caesar to do this.

Caesar and Curio

As the year 51 wore on, Caelius did his duty to Cicero, sending him
frequent reports of the latest developments. Marcellus had failed to get
anywhere yet with the plan to recall Caesar. The date he was trying for was
1 March 50. Caesar used the main political blocking tactic to prevent this
happening—tribunes, in particular a young man called Curio, who had at
first sided with the *optimates* and later gone over to Caesar.

Curio served Caesar well, and 1 March 50 passed without Caesar's recall. Caelius continued to keep Cicero informed, but there is a distinct impression at times that Cicero did not really come to grips with what was happening. He was quite busily occupied in the province, and his forces had fought a successful engagement against the Parthians on its border. He captured a small town called Pindinessus, though he was aware that it hardly ranked as a major military success. (' "What on earth is Pindinessus?", you will ask. "Who *are* these people? I've never even heard of them!" ', he wrote to Atticus in December 51.) But he could be saluted as an *Imperator*, and in fact became very anxious to have official recognition of his achievements. Perhaps the concern he felt over this matter (especially when Cato started to block his claim for a 'triumph') blinded him to the bitter struggle taking place in Rome. By now no one in the city was talking about partnerships, at least where Caesar and Pompey were concerned. It was apparent that the split between the two was final, and that Pompey was beginning to be accepted by the Senate, if not with enthusiasm, at least as the lesser of the two evils.

The attempt to recall Caesar continued

By June 50, Cicero was beginning to realise the serious nature of the position. He replied to Caelius' news as follows:

> 'I'm worried about the way things are going in Rome ... I should still like you to send me a letter which I can get on my way home (since my year of office will be over by the time you receive this), which will explain the whole political situation to me. Otherwise I shall feel like a regular "country mouse" when I come to the city. You're the best person for the job!' [Cicero, *ad Fam.* II 12]

Cicero left his province on the earliest possible date. He has often been accused of acting rather irresponsibly in this, since he knew that there was no one with the experience needed to whom he could safely entrust Cilicia. But his first thoughts were for getting back home.

Caelius did continue to write, and a letter written in the month of June tried to explain the latest manoeuvres involving Caesar, Pompey and Curio:

> 'On the question of politics, everything depends on one thing—the provinces. So far, Pompey seems to be acting with the Senate, arguing that Caesar *should* retire from Gaul—on 13 November. Curio is dead set on stopping this, and has abandoned all his other ideas.' [Cicero, *ad Fam.* VIII 11]

In September, Caelius wrote again:

'The crucial thing is this (and this is what will be fought by those in power): Pompey is determined not to let Caesar be consul unless he first gives up his army and provinces. Caesar is sure that he can only be safe if he hangs on to his army, but he's suggesting a compromise —namely that both Pompey and he should give up their armies. So all that old "friendship" (the partnership we hated) hasn't just become frayed at the edges; open war is breaking out.' [Cicero, *ad Fam.* VIII 14]

By this time, then, it was becoming evident, at least to those close to the centre of events, that there was a real danger of civil war. Although Curio was still working for Caesar, Pompey was now definitely backing the proposal to get Caesar recalled on 13 November 50.

This was the situation Cicero found when he returned to Italy at last, in November. Although his distance had stopped him seeing the threat of war as clearly as he would have done had he been in Rome, when he came back he understood the grave nature of the situation. In fact, he decided it would be best if he didn't go to Rome immediately. By 13 November Pompey and the Senate had *still* not managed to pass the bill to recall Caesar. Curio's year of office ended on 9 December, and some of the Senate must have thought that now their chance had come. But Caesar had two tribunes ready to step into Curio's shoes, one of whom was Mark Antony. Their intention was plain: they would continue to veto any suggestion that Caesar should be brought back from Gaul, before he had secured the consulship for 48. Caesar still hoped to stand in absence.

Cicero's view of the crisis

After Cicero's return to Italy, he wrote frequently to Rome about the situation. He met Pompey in December, but the meeting did not give him much to cheer about. A very important letter soon after this meeting gives the full picture of what he was thinking:

To Atticus at Rome   Formiae,
                                                                18 December 50

'You mention that people are extremely interested in my return, and that all the good, loyal citizens (and even those who are fairly loyal) are sure how I shall act. But really, I don't even know who these "loyalists" are. Certainly there is no *class* that is loyal, only individuals. But if there is a split, we need a class, or party. Is the Senate loyal, when it leaves provinces with nobody to govern them? Or the tax-collectors, whom we could never really rely on, and who are now in with Caesar? The *equites*, then? Or the farmers, who want peace at all costs? Are *they* going to be afraid of a tyrant's rule, when they have never objected to one provided they were left in peace? Well then, do I approve of the fact that a man is to be allowed to stand for the consulship when he has held on to his army longer than he was allowed to? No, I don't, and nor do I like the idea of his standing in absence. But in granting him one of these, we give the other. Did I think it was a good thing to allow him ten years of military command, or approve of the way this was carried out? If I did, I should have been approving of my own banishment! ...

The reason for all our troubles is simple: we should have resisted him when he was weak. Now he (Caesar) has eleven legions, as much cavalry as he wants, the people north of the river Po, the city crowds, and all those tribunes and corrupt young men—and he himself is a commander of the greatest distinction and courage. We have to fight him, or let him stand. "Fight", perhaps you say. "It's that or becoming slaves". What's the use? If we lose, we'll be exiles, if we win, slaves anyway. "Well, what *can* you do, then?" I *suppose* I'll act like an animal —when in trouble, make for my own kind. Like a cow joining the herd, I'll join up with those you call the "loyalists", even if they are rushing to their ruin. It's such a mess, but I can still see the right course. ...

I've gone on and on about the political situation. I could go on longer, but my lamp is running out. This, then, is my verdict. "Marcus Tullius Cicero, give your vote." "My vote is for Pompey— that is, it's for you, Pomponius Atticus".' [Cicero, *ad Att.* VII 7]

6

Civil War and the Final Stand

The Senate's Ultimate Decree

On 4 January 49, Cicero reached Rome. He had had a letter from Caesar asking him to try for peace, but could do nothing. Later he wrote to a friend and said:

> 'I could get nowhere. I had arrived too late, I was alone; people thought I didn't understand the case. I found that I had come back to a madhouse, where everyone was thirsting for war.' [Cicero, *ad Fam.* XVI 12]

Caesar, while not afraid of war, *had* tried to get peace. In fact at one point it was clear from a vote in the Senate that the great majority of senators wished to avoid war, even if it meant making concessions to Caesar. A compromise solution had been approved by 370 votes to 22. These 22, the really hard core of the *optimates*, determined not to give in to Caesar, and blocked the proposal. But for this, the Civil War might have been avoided. As it was, Caesar's demands were not met, and when he himself continued to use Mark Antony to prevent his recall, the Senate passed the Ultimate Decree (used last in 63 against Catiline). It was 7 January, and Caesar's two tribunes left Rome to meet Caesar at Ravenna. At the start of his own account of the Civil War, Caesar wrote as follows:

> The Senate now turned to their last resort, the Ultimate Decree. Never before had this been used except in dire emergencies, when the city had been almost destroyed by sheer violence and the misuse of power.... At this moment Caesar was at Ravenna, waiting for a reply to the very mild requests he had made, and hoping that the people would have enough sense of justice to enable the matter to be settled peacefully. [Caesar, *de Bello Civili* I 5]

There is a good example of how the same event can be interpreted by different sides in very different ways. Cicero wrote:

'The situation is that our old friend Caesar has sent the Senate a letter, both bitter and threatening. He's still so insolent that he's holding on to his army and province against the Senate's will.' [Cicero, *ad Fam*. XVI II]

Pompey had taken advantage of the increasing fear of Caesar, and had now emerged as the defender of the Senate—a slightly ironic turn of fate, when one considers his relations with them at earlier points of his career. But perhaps in his heart, Pompey had never wanted to be hated or feared by the *optimates*. There have been signs throughout that what he sought was to be recognised as the *princeps senatus* (the leading citizen in the Senate—and in the State), a man who could command the highest possible respect and influence; the Republic's hero, not its destroyer.

Crossing the Rubicon

When Caesar's tribunes, Antony and Cassius, reached him at Ravenna, Caesar immediately started gathering his forces for the attack. The decisive move has been told by many writers. It took place on 11 January 49, and Appian, a writer from the second century AD, will tell it:

> Caesar decided to take the initiative in the great war by using his single legion of 5000 men (all he had with him at the time) against key points of Italy, first of all. . . . When he reached the river Rubicon,

22. *The legionary eagles and standards*

the boundary between Gaul and Italy, and looked out across the stream, he was deep in thought, considering all the trouble which would follow if he and his army went across this river. Then he came to himself, and said to his friends, "If I don't cross this river, it will be the start of much distress for me; if I cross it, there will be distress for everyone". These words put an end to his doubts—and he crossed over, crying out as he did so, "*Alea iacta est*" ("The die is cast"). [Appian, *Bellum civile* II 34]

This really was war. By crossing into Italy with armed forces, Caesar was in effect making a declaration of war against the State. The trigger that had jerked Caesar into action was the Ultimate Decree of the Senate. But what really caused the war? Was the clash inevitable, or could one side have climbed down? Who should be blamed? There are no easy answers to these questions, and we leave it to each reader to decide for himself where to pin the blame, and whether there was an alternative.

Which side to join?

Decisions, of a different kind, were needed by Romans living at the time. Cicero had declared his vote—to Atticus at least. Everyone was involved. The legionaries, the small farmers, or the unemployed in the city, would not have considered the complicated political principles which Cicero discussed. These might be led on by the hope of personal security, or a sense of loyalty to their army-commander. We have no record of the way in which they reached their decision. As in all matters of Roman history, the point of view which comes down to us is that of the well-off, the influential. Their thinking we *can* examine. Apart from considerations of loyalty, men in the Senate or *equites* would have given careful thought to their own career prospects; they would have asked themselves which side was more likely to introduce the type of government they themselves wanted. Nor could they rule out the question of which would be more lenient to defeated opponents, in the event of victory.

Whatever one thought, it would have been practically impossible to sit on the fence. Civil War catches even the most detached in its grip. Cicero chose the Senate. Any other line would have been a reversal of views expressed numerous times, in speeches, letters and philosophical works. But his letters show that his commitment was far from enthusiastic. Immediately after Caesar crossed the Rubicon, Cicero began a frantic correspondence (principally with Atticus), often writing a long letter every day. A few extracts will show his mood in the first few days of the war:

(12 January, to Tiro) . . . 'On the whole, our side are starting to make active preparations at last, thanks to the energy and influence of our friend Pompey—who, now that it's too late, is starting to be afraid of Caesar. . . .'

(17 January, to Atticus) . . . 'I don't know what plan Pompey has thought of, or *is* thinking of. . . . If he makes a stand in Italy, we shall all be together; if he leaves Italy, I really shall have to think again. . . .'

(19 January, to Atticus). . . . 'What *is* going on? I'm completely in the dark . . . .'

(22 January, to Atticus) . . . 'Can I commit myself wholly to Pompey's side? . . . . He has absolutely no plan, and completely rejects all my advice. Should I try to stall, then, and avoid committing myself, so that I can join whichever side wins power? . . .' [Cicero, *Letters* passim]

Cicero and the Senatorial side

Cicero took a post in the Senatorial army, though with reluctance. Italy was divided into areas, and he was put in charge of Capua (see map p. 19). His firm opinion was that it would be disastrous for Pompey to abandon Italy. Pompey, however, was relying on the fact that he had massive support in the East (as a result of his campaigns in the sixties), and also in Spain. This increased Cicero's dissatisfaction. To add to his problems, several of his friends, such as Caelius, were urging him to join Caesar. Cicero also retained his high regard for Caesar's talents, and was fiercely critical of the Senate's leaders (as he had often been before the war). There was much to tempt him to give up working for Pompey's cause:

1 March 49. We are still waiting for the news from Brundisium. (*Pompey had headed there in preparation for sailing East.*) If Caesar has caught up with Pompey, there is a slight chance of peace; but if Pompey has already crossed over, the war will be ruinous. [Cicero, *ad Att.* VIII 13]

But when the news came that Pompey *had* crossed over, Cicero's attitude suddenly changed. He started to regret that he had not stuck with Pompey more firmly, however badly the Senate had managed the cause. After another three months of hesitation and inaction, he eventually sailed to join Pompey in his camp. However, this only renewed and reinforced his bitterness, since he was not well received, and disliked the violent and extremist ideas being put forward by some of the *optimates*.

Pharsalus and the death of Pompey

It would not be possible to give here the details of the war. (Caesar's own commentary is full and illuminating.) The most important victory was won by Caesar in 48, at Pharsalus, in central Greece. It was a resounding triumph, brilliantly conceived and fought against superior numbers. (Cicero himself was not there: he had been left at Dyrrachium, unwell.) After the defeat, Pompey escaped from Greece and made his way to Egypt, trusting in old friends there. But on his arrival he was murdered, perhaps because the Egyptians did not wish to be associated with the losing side.

The war had allowed Pompey to gain, for a short time, his highest ambition—to be recognised as the military leader of the Senate. But he achieved this at the expense of breaking completely his former partnership with Caesar, and eventually at the expense of his own life. Cicero, for all the ties which had so often linked him to Pompey, wasted little breath in mourning his death:

> 'I never had any doubt how Pompey would end. People everywhere had so completely lost faith in his chances of success that it seemed likely that this would happen wherever he tried to land. I can't help feeling sorry he's dead. I know that he was an honest, decent and upright man.' [Cicero, *ad Att.* xi 6]

Cicero's return to Italy

After Pharsalus, in October 48, Cicero sailed back to Italy and stayed at Brundisium. Later he wrote to Atticus to say that he had never regretted leaving the camp, because there was so much cruelty: they were considering outlawing whole classes, not merely individuals. His part in the war was a strange mixture. In a way he had showed strength, since the temptations to join Caesar were very strong. Caesar had gone so far as to visit him to try to persuade him to side with him, but Cicero had said that he had much to say in defence of Pompey. Caesar told him he didn't want *that* sort of talk. No doubt he could still fear the magic of Cicero's tongue.

The period after Pharsalus was not a happy one for Cicero. His return to Brundisium showed that he was assuming the war was virtually over. But the Senate fought on, and for a time things looked bad for Caesar, now engaged in campaigns in Egypt. Cicero began to have a nasty suspicion that the Pompeian forces might after all win, despite the death of Pompey. If so, his position, as one who had in effect abandoned the Senate's cause, would be decidedly unpleasant.

He was also troubled by private worries. There had been a serious

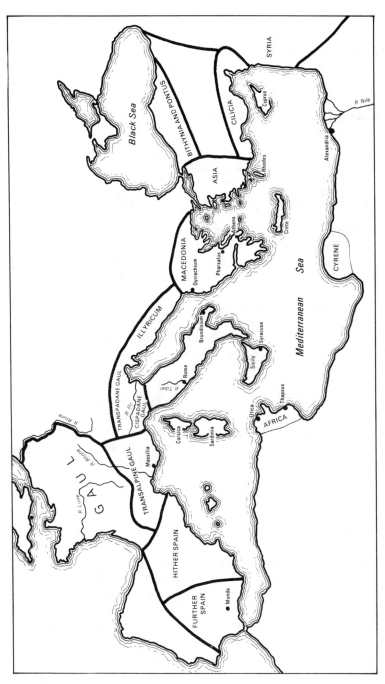

23. *The Roman Empire in the time of Cicero*

quarrel with his brother Quintus, which lasted well into 47, with Quintus blaming his elder brother for the stand he had taken against Caesar. Also, his marriage to Terentia, which had lasted over thirty years, began to run into difficulties, and early in 46 they were divorced. (The trouble had been money, and Cicero had been writing to Atticus on the subject very indignantly.) Nor were these the only members of his family causing him anxiety. His daughter's second marriage was going very badly, and she herself was in ill-health.

Cicero reconciled with Caesar

But Caesar's cause was not in fact going so badly, and the trouble in Alexandria was decisively overcome. He followed this up with a lightning campaign in Asia Minor. (*'Veni, vidi, vici'*: 'I came, I saw, I conquered'.) Then, in September 47, he returned to Italy. Cicero was still at Brundisium, and on hearing of his arrival, hurried to meet him. The relief caused by this encounter must have been tremendous. For, Plutarch says:

> 'When Caesar saw him coming towards him, a long way in front of everyone else, he got down, embraced him, and continued along the road with him for several hundred yards, talking to him privately. From this time on, he always treated Cicero kindly and with respect. [Plutarch, *Life of Cicero* 39]

Cicero, free from fear at last, could return again to Rome. There he took his place in the Senate, though rather uneasily, in view of his rather odd situation in regard to Caesar. (He could never betray his political ideas altogether, so that even if Caesar wanted him to use his powers of oratory in his cause, he remained silent.) As in the period 56-1, he turned to writing. Much of his work was on philosophical subjects, and it became extremely popular in later historical periods.

The end of the war

The war continued. Despite the continuing resistance, Caesar was beginning to put into practice some of his political ideas. But he was not in Rome long enough to get very far, and in the early months of 46 had to fight another important battle against the Pompeian troops—who are now often called the 'Republicans', since they were those who fought on to preserve the old Republic against the revolution of Caesar. The Republicans put up a brave showing, but on 6 April 46, at Thapsus in North Africa, were again defeated. The most notable casualty was Cato, for so long the leader of the *optimates*: he committed suicide shortly after the

battle. His courage and idealism made him a martyr—and
work in praise of him, which so annoyed Caesar that he r
pamphlet called 'Anti-Cato'. Even then, the war was not ove
not until 17 March 45, at Munda in Spain, that the last Repub
was defeated.

During this period, Caesar was officially *dictator*. He first recei   ne

24. *Coin of Caesar struck by him while dictator*

title in 49, though he held it for only eleven days. In 48 he was again made
dictator, for a year. In 46, he received the position for ten years. After the
final clearing-up of the opposition he returned to the city late in 45, and
started to work for the restoration of order. Cicero was clearly unhappy
at the power Caesar had, but came to believe that his only useful role was
to urge Caesar to save the Republic. This he did, in his first major speech
for some time. During this, he dealt with a rumour that Caesar might be
assassinated. Caesar was reported to have said that he was not greatly
bothered—an attitude which led Cicero to profess horror, which he may
indeed have felt. He still cared for the Republic, and argued that if Caesar

were to die, the Republic would have no chance of survival. (Those plotting Caesar's downfall were saying the exact opposite: there was no hope of the Republic's survival *unless* Caesar died.)

Caesar's plans for Rome

Gradually, more and more people realised that Caesar had no intention of going back to the old Republic, no intention of giving up his own position. (A famous quotation of his was that 'Sulla didn't know his political ABC when he gave up the dictatorship'.) He was also causing great offence to the Senate by his high-handed treatment of things which they still felt were important. The worst example of this came at the end of 45, when one of the consuls died. Cicero wrote to a friend in a state of great indignation:

> 'Shortly after noon, Caesar appointed as consul a man to hold office until 1 January 44—the following morning! So you will see that while Caninius was consul no one even had lunch. But at least there were no serious disasters during his consulship. In fact, he was an astonishingly watchful consul, since he didn't have a wink of sleep in his whole consulship. This will seem like a great joke to you. But you're not here—if you were, you'd weep.' [Cicero, *ad Fam.* VII 30]

During the few months he was in Rome, Caesar worked with great energy, achieving notable reforms in many areas. (For example, the Roman calendar, which had been in a chaotic state.) He tackled bribery in the courts, tried to strengthen the Senate (though here too he gave offence, by allowing 'lower classes' to become senators), brought the elections under control, took steps to deal with economic problems (debt and the corn dole for the unemployed), planned to rebuild the city, increased the penalties for crime, and in general showed himself a practical politician with an eye for social needs that was shared by few of his contemporaries. But he did not overcome the hatred of his opponents. Indeed, some of his measures were greeted by the Senate with disapproval, as a threat to their own power and wealth.

Perhaps the final straw, the thing that pushed the opposition into the action which had long been rumoured, was Caesar's taking the title *dictator perpetuus* (dictator for life), which he did at the beginning of 44. Up till that time it was possible to cling to a hope, however faint, that Caesar was not intending to hold on to power for ever. But now, with the Civil War finished, he was taking a title which showed that he regarded himself as a single ruler, and that he was going to remain one. This must have drained away the last drop of hope that the Republic would be

25. *Reconstruction of the Temple of Julius Caesar*

brought back. To be *dictator* for life was a contradiction in terms: dictators were set up for a crisis, and only for that purpose. There were even stories that Caesar planned to go still further, and have himself crowned *rex* (king). But kings, as Caesar knew, were regarded at Rome as tyrants. The last king, Tarquin the Proud, had been expelled by Brutus in 509 BC, to set up the Republic. Caesar even said on one occasion '*Non sum rex, sed Caesar*' ('I am nót a king, I'm Caesar'). Although other actions might have suggested that he was at least considering the idea, this is not the vital question, though it is an interesting one. The fact was that, whatever title Caesar took, he was not going to abandon his power.

The Ides of March

This was the background to the famous events of 15 March 44. Through Shakespeare's *Julius Caesar*, they have become familiar to many who know nothing of the political reasons for the assassination. Shakespeare based his work on the account of Plutarch, and although it was written over one hundred years after the event, the basic facts are well enough confirmed, even if some of the details are less definitely historical:

> Caesar entered, and the Senate rose to honour him. Some of the conspirators took up positions behind his chair, others went to meet him. They pretended to be supporting a plea being made by Tillius

79

Cimber for his exiled brother. As Caesar went to his chair, they all accompanied him, making appeals to him. Caesar sat down, and continued to refuse what they asked. They persisted, and when they would not stop, Caesar began to get angry. Tillius then grabbed hold of his toga, using both hands. He pulled the toga down, the signal to start the attack.

Casca struck the first blow, wounding Caesar in the neck with his dagger. It was not a fatal blow—not even very deep, since Casca no doubt was very nervous at the start of this daring deed. So Caesar was able to turn and grip the knife, holding on to it. As he did so, both he and Casca shouted out—Caesar called in Latin: 'You scoundrel, Casca, what are you up to?', and Casca in Greek: 'Help, brother'.

This was how it started. Those who weren't in on the conspiracy were quite amazed and horrified—so much so that they were too afraid either to run away or to help Caesar—too afraid even to speak. The others, those who had come prepared to kill, bared their daggers, surrounding Caesar completely. Wherever he turned, he met dagger-blows, and saw the naked steel pointing at his face and eyes. Driven this way and that, like a wild animal caught in a net, he was forced to suffer at the hands of each one—they had agreed that all must share the sacrifice, and taste blood. It was because of this agreement that even Brutus struck him, in the groin. It is said that against all the others Caesar fought back, moving swiftly this way and that to dodge the blows, and crying for help. But when he saw that Brutus had drawn his dagger, he covered his face with his toga, and fell to the ground. It might have been chance, or he may have been pushed by his assassins, but in either case the place he fell was up against the pedestal on which stood the statue of Pompey. The pedestal was stained with blood; it was as if Pompey himself were looking down over this act of revenge against his old enemy, as he lay there at his feet, struggling and writhing with so many wounds.
[Plutarch, *Life of Caesar* 66]

Why Caesar was killed

The deed was done. It had been planned and carried out by men who had refused to see the Republic they had loved destroyed by one man. Not all of them had always hated Caesar. In fact, the connexion between Brutus and Caesar had been particularly close—which is why Caesar was especially sad to see him among the conspirators: 'Even you, Brutus?' ('*Et tu, Brute?*'), he was rumoured to have said—at least according to Shakespeare. The assassins were sincere men, and they regarded themselves as 'the Liberators'—Brutus was proud of his descent from that other Brutus who

26. *Coin of Brutus and the liberators* (reverse: *Cap of Liberty*)

had expelled the tyrant. What they stood for was *Libertas*—'freedom'. But it was a very restricted kind of freedom. It was certainly not freedom for the whole people of Rome. The issue was not one of 'tyranny' versus 'democracy'. The freedom they wanted was the freedom to gain as much power as possible for themselves, the traditional ruling class of Rome, the *nobiles*, with their long lines of consuls, their ancient control of the Senate.

27. *Brutus*

F

They had ideals, but it would be wrong to think that they were necessarily, or even likely to be, the men who would solve Rome's economic or social problems. Look back over the past twenty years, and the history of the *optimates'* attitude to reform, and it is clear that the ordinary people of Rome were not going to assume that the death of the 'tyrant' was very good news to them. As it happened, they did not think this, and Caesar's friends were immediately able to get an enormous amount of public sympathy. The 'Liberators' found that, so far from being popular heroes, they were disliked intensely.

What had Cicero's place in all these events been? He was not in the plot. Plutarch gives a reason for this, which may well be the true one: the conspirators thought he was too timid a character. He may well have seen the murder, and his political sympathies were certainly with those who carried it out. But Cicero was alarmed at the state of affairs which resulted.

The two people who came out of the incident in the strongest position were Mark Antony, Caesar's right-hand man since his tribunate in 49, and a young man called Octavian, only eighteen at the time of Caesar's death. Antony must have been considerably peeved to discover that the young Octavian, Caesar's grand-nephew, had been named as his chief heir. The young man had obviously impressed his great-uncle greatly, and became the adopted son of the dead dictator. In March 44, no one in Rome could have dreamt that Octavian would be the one who would emerge, after thirteen more years of civil war, as sole ruler of the Roman Empire, that he would succeed where his 'father' had failed, and that he would take command of Rome for forty-five years, introducing a long period of almost uninterrupted peace.

Cicero and Antony

Cicero now had eighteen months to live, and they were to prove among the most eventful of his life. His own circumstances had not been free from trouble in the preceding year. The bitterest tragedy was the death of his daughter Tullia, which he took deeply to heart, and over which he could not be consoled. He had remarried after the divorce of Terentia, but quickly divorced his second wife also, taking his revenge on her for failing to grieve sufficiently over the death of his 'Tulliola'. Although literary activities continued to be his main comfort, he could not ignore politics, nor did he wish to.

When Antony took command of events in Rome, Cicero quickly decided that his presence meant that in a sense the conspirators had failed.

28. *Mark Antony*

They were in fact forced to leave Rome. One of them wrote to others in the plot two days after the death of Caesar, as follows:

> 'Do you want to know what my advice is? I think we must give in to fate—clear out of Italy and live in Rhodes or somewhere. If things start to improve, we can return to Rome; if they remain as they are, we can stay in exile; if they get worse, we shall have to take extreme measures.' [Cicero, *ad Fam.* XI 1]

Antony cashed in on the public sympathy for Caesar, reading out to the crowds the will of Caesar (it contained a sum of money for each citizen), and burning his body in public, in the Forum. Cicero was violently annoyed. He was out of Rome, and decided he had to stay out. Atticus, who as always steered clear of the political troubles, was in the city, and there was another feverish burst of correspondence between the two. Cicero wrote on 18 April 44: 'Good grief! The tyrant may be dead, but the tyranny is certainly not!' Four days later he wrote again, in similar vein:

> 'Oh Atticus, I'm afraid that all we have got out of the events of 15 March was a thrill of pleasure, and a way of satisfying our hatred. What news I hear from Rome, and what things I see here! "It was a glorious deed, but only half-complete."' [Cicero, *ad Att.* XIV 12]

The letters continued in a constant stream. We can follow through them the smallest changes—always magnified by Cicero, who saw a small alteration in the situation as reason for great hope or depression. For several months there was uncertainty. Could any settlement be made to satisfy Antony and the supporters of Caesar on the one hand, and Brutus and the 'Republicans' on the other? Cicero blamed Brutus for not acting boldly enough against Antony. By June he started to hope that the young Octavian might save the situation, if he could be kept from becoming too close to Antony.

Octavian

As the year wore on, however, Octavian was starting to make his own move. His position was a more complicated one than that of Antony or the conspirators, since he could threaten Antony's control of the pro-Caesar support, and was obviously bound to oppose the assassins of Caesar. (He was using the name Caesar as a way of strengthening his own position, and was actually recruiting an army of his own.) Cicero wanted to support him, but was not sure that he could. In November, he wrote to Atticus and told him that Octavian was writing to him every day, urging him to take a hand to save the Republic again. But he couldn't decide, and while he hesitated, war broke out between Antony and the conspirators, whose forces were split. Antony decided to take on Decimus Brutus, a conspirator, then in charge of Cisalpine Gaul. He appointed himself governor of the province in Decimus' place, and left Rome on 28 November 44, to besiege his forces in Mutina (see map of Italy on p. 19). This action finally prompted Cicero to act himself, and from December 44 onwards, he became once again the leader in Rome of the Senatorial party. He turned his oratory, for long dormant, against the hated Mark Antony. The speeches he wrote were called the 'Philippics', after speeches by the Greek orator Demosthenes, whom he admired so much.

On 20 December 44, Cicero delivered his fourth Philippic. Antony was consul—for another eleven days. After his year, Cicero intended to have him declared a public enemy. He planned to use Octavian to secure his ends, and when the debate opened at the start of 43, the Senate were asked to recognise as legal the armies of Decimus and Octavian. Octavian was granted extraordinary powers for one of his age. Cicero thought he knew how to handle the young man—he had defeated Catiline before Octavian was even born! Octavian, whose claims to be in command of an army were extremely dubious, played along with Cicero for the time being.

Cicero leads the Senate

In the following months, Cicero displayed an incredible energy. He had set himself the task of rallying the Senate's forces, and worked at the job with all the zeal he had shown against Catiline. It should not be forgotten that he was now sixty-three years old. He was dedicated to one end—the destruction of Antony, and with it, he hoped, the return of normal government. Without thinking out too clearly what sort of Republic it might be, he still believed in it. Moreover, he now had the chance to exert the influence in keeping with his position as a senior consular, which he had felt cheated of during the years of the 'Triumvirate'. He had an audience for his speeches, and a respect he had not known since the golden days of 63. He did not waste the opportunity. The Philippics continued to pour from his lips, letters (to all points of the compass) poured from his pen. On 2 February 43, war was declared on Antony. The focal point of the war was Mutina, and in April two battles were fought over the town. In the first, Antony faced the two consuls; he defeated one, but came out of it in the worse position against the other. On 21 April, Decimus made a break from the besieged town, and won a clear victory over Antony, forcing him to escape. Both consuls died as a result of the battle, and Antony escaped from Mutina to the other side of the Alps.

Cicero was in high spirits. He believed the war to be practically over, and started to work for a peaceful future. One step was to ensure that Octavian did not become too powerful, and Cicero began to try to check his position. But he was being over-confident. For one thing, Antony's forces were far from defeated, and for another, Octavian was not going to take Cicero's treatment of him lying down.

By the end of May, Antony was on the borders of Italy, recruiting fresh forces. Octavian was becoming more and more dissatisfied with the way the Senate were acting, and seized on the death of the two consuls in the battle of Mutina to press his own claims. (He was now nineteen).

Brutus and Cicero

One man who was very unhappy about the way Cicero was planning his tactics was the assassin, Marcus Brutus. In a letter to Atticus, he criticised Cicero severely for boosting the young man so much, warning that Octavian could be another tyrant as easily as Antony. In a long attack on Cicero's policy, he argued that he was being blind to the realities of the situation:

'I know that all Cicero has done has been done with the best of intentions. I have experienced his great loyalty to the Republic, and can appreciate it. . . . But all I can say is this: what he *has* done is to encourage, not check, the ambition and desire for power of this youth.' [Cicero, *ad Brut.* 1 17]

He concludes by saying:

'If I were not as fond of Cicero as he seems to think Octavian is of him, I should not have written to you like this. It upsets me to think that you will be angry to read this, since you are so attached to your friends, especially Cicero. But believe me, I like Cicero as much as ever—it's his point of view I can't respect so much now.' [*Ibid.*]

Of course the criticisms reached Cicero, who replied thoughtfully and fully. It is almost the last of the more than 900 letters to and from Cicero which have survived from his lifetime, and is a dignified attempt to justify his action and position:

'You will remember, Brutus, that after the death of Caesar, on that famous 15 March of yours, I complained that you had omitted to do something, and warned that there was a storm threatening the Republic. . . . When I returned to Rome, I immediately stood up against the wickedness and madness of Antony. This turned him against me, and so I started to think of a really Brutus-like plan to set the Republic free (this is what your family is so good at doing!).

The rest of the story is too long to go over, and since it concerns my own actions, I will say nothing of it. All I will mention is this: the young Octavian's actions are like a river flowing from my advice— and it is to *him* that we owe the fact that we survive. I agree that I voted for honours for him, but they had to be voted, and he deserved them. For, when we first started to feel free again, and even before Decimus had confirmed this by his great bravery, this lad was the only person who could save us from Antony. This being so, how could we have offered him too much?' [Cicero, *ad Brut.* 1 15]

Octavian joins Antony

But Cicero's confidence that Octavian would save them from Antony *was* misplaced. Twelve years later, after continued civil strife, Octavian *did* save Rome from Antony, and Rome was duly grateful. But the hour for this was not yet. Octavian was not going to be sacrificed to Cicero's vaguely thought-out plans. He wanted to be consul, and on 19 August, despite the Senate's opposition, he got what he wanted. As usual in these things, the matter was decided not in the Senate House, but by the army.

29. *Octavian*

After becoming consul, Octavian's tactics took another turn: the bills that had made Antony, and his partner Lepidus, outlaws were cancelled. They returned to Italy, and at the end of October met Octavian. The result of the conference was that the differences between Octavian and Antony were buried. They united to oppose the last remnants of the 'Republic'. A list of the leading Republicans was published. In view of the Philippics, it is no surprise to learn that Cicero's name was on the list. (Octavian did not oppose Antony's wish on this.) The purpose of the list was the same as that of Sulla's 'proscriptions' nearly forty years earlier—the men named were to die.

The Final scene

Cicero was not in Rome—he had left for his villa at Tusculum. His brother Quintus was with him, but returned to Rome, hoping to raise money to enable them to escape to Greece. He didn't get that far. Together with his son, he was executed. Cicero could still have got away. He got on his ship, but only went as far as his other villa, near Formiae. There was not much to be gained by exile for an old man, who knew there could be no way back this time.

At this point, it would be possible to pause and look back over the life of Cicero—to try to answer many of the intriguing questions which it raises, both about the man himself and what he stood for. How important *was* he? Was he a failure? Was he consistent, honest, unscrupulous? Were his hopes and ideals all pipedreams, or did he have an idea which could have given a solution to Rome's political troubles? What values did he stand for? What did he mean by the 'Republic'? Many books have been written, many judgements have been made about his character. Someone has said that the judgements tell us more about the person who makes them than they do about Cicero. It would be easy to treat Cicero harshly.

30. *Cicero*

But two things must be borne in mind particularly, when trying to assess his life and career. One is that standards change. Possibly, even, they improve. At any rate, there is no point in taking Cicero outside his own society and judging him against the ideas of a completely different civilisation. The other is that Cicero's complete frankness, especially in writing to Atticus, makes him open to attack in a way which most of us, and most of the politicians of his day, are protected from. Despair, fear, uncertainty, are feelings shared by very many people. Most of them do not put them down on paper as fully as Cicero did, and even if they do, they cannot normally be read 2000 years later.

These two points should not blind us to Cicero's faults. They were visible to his contemporaries, too. But they were only a part of the picture. As we have seen, there was much to be said on the other side. So there will be no long obituary of Cicero, no summing up of his achievements or character. Instead, Plutarch will have the final word, as (in his life of Cicero, chaps. 47-9) he describes the final scene in Cicero's long and colourful life. The date was 7 December 43. Cicero was just short of sixty-four years old. He had arrived at his villa, and went in to see if he could sleep. His slaves had decided that it was not safe for him to stay there, and placed him on his sedan-chair, intending to carry him back to his ship.

> In the meantime, however, the murderers had arrived. They were the centurion Herennius and an officer, Popillius, whom Cicero had once defended on the charge of murdering his father. They had soldiers with them. The doors were shut against them, but they battered them down. But they could not find Cicero, and the people in the house denied any knowledge of where he was. Then a young man, one who had been educated in literature and philosophy by Cicero, and had been a slave, but was given his citizenship by Cicero's brother Quintus, spoke up. He told Herennius that Cicero was being carried down to the sea by his slaves, along a path through the woods. Popillius with a few men went down to the place where the path emerged, while Herennius ran down the path after him. Cicero heard him coming, and ordered the slaves to put down the chair. He sat there, his chin resting on his left hand, in a position he often adopted, and looked straight at his murderers. He was dusty, and his hair disarranged, while his face was pinched and furrowed, from all the troubles it had seen. Most of those who stood by covered their faces with their hands at the fatal moment. He stretched his head and neck forward from his seat, and his throat was cut. He was in his sixty-fourth year. Herennius, on the orders of Antony, cut off his head and hands—those hands which had written the Philippics.

When the parts of his body which had been cut off were brought to Rome, Antony was organising the elections. He heard the news, and when he saw the sight cried out: 'Now we will be able to stop all these killings.' Then he ordered the head and hands to be fastened up over the public platform. The sight made Romans shudder. It

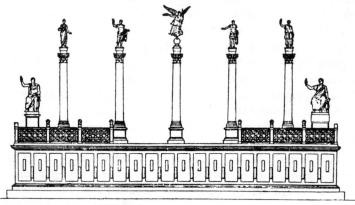

31. *The public platform, where Cicero's head and hands were hung*

was not the face of Cicero they seemed to see, but the very image of Antony's soul. . . .

A long time after this, Octavian (now the emperor Augustus) was visiting a grandson. The boy was holding a book of Cicero's in his hand. He was afraid of what Augustus might think of this, so he tried to hide it under his cloak. Augustus saw the book, and took it from him. He stood there and read most of it. Afterwards he handed the book back to the boy with the words: 'My child, Cicero was a wise man, and he loved his country well.'

Appendix 1

Glossary of Latin terms used

Cursus Honorum The ladder of public offices which Romans who were ambitious politically had to try to climb. The offices were:

Quaestor The first step. Held at a minimum age of 30, it was the passport to the Senate in Cicero's day, when there were twenty elected each year. (Like the other offices, it could be held for only one year.) Two were in charge of the Treasury in Rome, and the others mainly assisted provincial governors.

Aedile Minimum age 37. There were four elected annually. It was not essential in the *cursus honorum*, but very useful in keeping one's name known, in view of the long gap between quaestor and praetor. There were various duties in the city, including supervising building, market regulations, public games, etc.

Praetor Minimum age 40. There were eight elected annually. Like the consuls, the praetors had power to command armies and summon assemblies. Their main duty was to preside over the law-courts, and after their year of office they would become provincial governors (propraetors).

Consul Minimum age 43. There were two a year. They were the chief public officials, taking power alternately for a month, with responsibilities for forming and carrying out public policy. After office, usually one became proconsul in command of a province, and then exerted great influence in the Senate as a *consularis* (man of consular rank).

Dictator An office set up only for exceptional crises, and held for a maximum of six months by an appointment in the Senate. It gave powers greater than even that of the consuls. Sulla held the office for two years, a new development, which paved the way for Caesar's extended use of it.

Equites	A class of wealthy citizens (with a property qualification) immediately below the Senate. It included particularly financiers such as the *publicani* (tax-collectors) and the ruling classes of Italian towns.
Novus homo	The first man in a family to hold a public office—applied particularly to the first to become consul, and contrasted with:
Nobiles	Members of families which had included at least one consul in their line. The traditional ruling families in Rome.
Optimates	Those members of the Senate, and supporters, who defended the established procedures and traditions in Roman political life, mainly because they saw that they could best achieve their own ambitions if there were no changes, and believed the Senate the most efficient and suitable body to control affairs.
Populares	Unlike the Optimates (with whom they were often contrasted) they preferred to work for their political ends—sometimes connected with social reform—through the popular Assemblies, rather than the Senate.
Tribuni plebis (tribunes)	There were ten elected annually. They did not have to have held a previous office, but it could be an alternative to the position of aedile on the *cursus honorum*. Originally they were set up to look after the interests of the *plebs* (plebeians) who were at one time less privileged than the patricians in Rome. They could pass decrees which counted as laws, could call the Senate, use their power of veto against other tribunes or officials, and were very useful to ambitious or powerful men as a way to avoid the Senate.

Appendix 2

The Principal Characters

Marcus Antonius (Mark Antony) — (c.82-30 BC) Quaestor in Gaul with Caesar in 51. Tribune in 49, defending Caesar's interests. In 44 consul with Caesar, and afterwards supported Caesar's party against Republicans. Joined with Octavian and Lepidus (the Second Triumvirate) in November 43— had Cicero killed in proscriptions. Eventually split with Octavian, united with Cleopatra in Egypt and committed suicide after defeat at Actium, by Octavian, in 31.

Titus Pomponius Atticus — (109-32 BC) Member of *equites*. Close friend of Cicero for many years. (Published Cicero's letters to him.) Named Atticus after long residence in Athens (to escape Sulla). Remained politically neutral and friendly to all sides, including Octavian, until his death.

Marcus Junius Brutus — (c.85-42 BC) Quaestor in Cilicia in 53. Joined Pompey in Civil War, but spared by Caesar after Pharsalus. In 44 was praetor, and leading member of plot to kill Caesar. Fought against Antony and Octavian. Committed suicide after losing battle of Philippi.

Gaius Julius Caesar — (c.102-44 BC) Opposed death-penalty for Catilinarians in 63. In 62 praetor, and propraetor in Spain. Consul in 59 (First Triumvirate with Pompey and Crassus). Commanded Gaul till 49. Civil War against Senate under Pompey. Assassinated 15 March 44.

Lucius Sergius Catilina (Catiline): — (?-62 BC) Lieutenant of Sulla in 80s. Stood against Cicero for consul in 64, unsuccessfully, and again in 63. Driven to conspiracy, but outmanoeuvred by Cicero, and defeated and killed in battle early 62.

Marcus Porcius Cato Uticensis — (95-46 BC) Proposed death-penalty for Catiline in 63. Uncompromising opponent of First Triumvirate, and of *populares*. Leading spokesman for *optimates*. In 58 sent to Cyprus, to remove his opposition, by Clodius. In Civil War followed Pompey, and committed suicide at Utica after defeat at Thapsus. (Hence name *Uticensis*.)

Publius Clodius — (?-52 BC) December 62 provoked political crisis by appearance at *Bona Dea* festival. In 59 transferred to plebeians. Tribune 58—outlawed Cicero. Later turned against Pompey, and lost support of Caesar because of gang-warfare against Milo. Killed by Milo's slaves 18 January 52.

Marcus Licinius Crassus Dives — (c.112-53 BC) Leader of businessmen through his property speculation. Extremely rich (*Dives* is Latin for 'The Rich'), and used wealth for political purposes (bribery, etc.). Defeated Spartacus' slave revolt in 72, but forced to share glory and consulship of 70 with rival, Pompey. Again joined Pompey and Caesar (First Triumvirate 60), and after second consulship (55), went to Syria as proconsul. Defeated and died at Carrhae (Parthians) in autumn 53.

Gaius Marius — (157-86 BC) Born near Arpinum (Cicero's town). Won consulship through military brilliance, shown in wars against African king Jugurtha. Civil War against Sulla—seized consulship for seventh time in 86, but died soon after.

Titus Annius Milo — (?-48 BC) Tribune 57, promoted Cicero's recall. Organised gladiators against Clodius' gangs. Avoided prosecution for violence, but exiled in 52 after Cicero had failed to defend him properly following murder of Clodius. Exiled at Massilia, and killed in 48.

Gaius Octavius (Octavian) — (62 BC-14 AD) Made heir of Caesar in his will. Gained illegal consulship in 43, aged 19. United with Antony and Lepidus (Second Triumvirate), but later fought Civil War against Antony, defeating him in 31. Became sole leader of Rome, taking title Augustus, and ruling till 14 AD.

Gnaeus Pompeius Magnus — (106-48 BC) Served with Sulla very successfully, winning title *Magnus* ('The Great'), and forcing Senate to give him extraordinary powers in wars in 70s. Forced his way to consulship with Crassus (70). Commands against pirates (67) and Mithridates (66). Joined Caesar and Crassus (First Triumvirate), and married Caesar's daughter. But after her death and that of Crassus, split with Caesar, leading Senate against him in Civil War. Killed in Egypt after defeat at Pharsalus, 48.

Lucius Cornelius Sulla	(138–78 BC) Won military renown fighting against *populares* (Marius) and Mithridates. Became *dictator* 81, and tried to strengthen Senate. (Killed many in proscriptions.) Retired in 79 and died a year later.

Index

aedileship (*aedile*), 21, 22, 55, 91

Antony (Marcus Antonius), 68, 70, 71, 82–87, 89, 90, 93

Arpinum, 12, 13, 18

Asia, 22, 23, 35, 36, 43, 44, 58, 76

Atticus (Titus Pomponius Atticus), 12, 16, 37–41, 43, 44, 46, 53, 57, 58, 64, 65, 67–69, 72–74, 76, 83–85, 89, 93

Bibulus (consul 59), 44–47

Britain, 58, 60

Brundisium, 50, 53, 74, 76

Brutus, Decimus, 84–86

Brutus, Marcus Junius (conspirator), 80, 81, 84–86, 93

Caelius, 64–68, 73

Caesar (Gaius Julius Caesar), 32, 33, 38, 40–49, 56–60, 62–74, 76–80, 82–84, 86, 93

Catiline (Lucius Sergius Catilina), 29–35, 44, 70, 84, 85, 93

Cato (Marcus Porcius Cato Uticensis), 33, 40, 41, 43, 44, 67, 76, 77, 93

Cicero (Marcus Tullius Cicero, the orator): letters, 11–12; background,
12–13; name, 13; education, 13–14; as orator, 15–17; quaestorship, 18; prosecution of Verres, 21; aedileship, 22; praetorship, 22–23; campaign for consulship, 24–26; consulship, 27–28; against Catiline, 29–33; relations with Pompey, 35–39; connexions with First Triumvirate, 40–44; opposition of Clodius, 45–58; in exile, 49–53; return to Rome, 54–56; position after Luca, 57–62; in Cilicia, 63–68; the Civil War, 69–76; position with regard to Caesar, 76–82; against Antony, 82–85; last stand, 85–87; death, 87–90

Cicero (Marcus Tullius Cicero, the son of the orator), 50, 51

Cicero (Quintus Tullius Cicero, brother of the orator), 24, 51–53, 55, 56, 58, 60, 76, 87, 89

Cilicia, 63–65, 67

Clodius (Publius Clodius), 38, 40, 45–49, 52–55, 60–62, 94

concordia ordinum (harmony of the Orders), 34–37, 39, 40

consulship (consul), 17, 19, 20, 22, 24–30, 40–44, 46, 54–56, 58, 60–63, 65, 66, 68, 69, 78, 81, 84–87, 91
Crassus (Marcus Licinius Crassus Dives), 20, 21, 39, 42, 43, 45, 47, 55–60, 94
Curio, 66–68
cursus honorum (ladder of office), 17, 21, 22, 91

dictatorship (dictator), 14, 36, 62, 77–79, 82, 91
Dyrrachium, 52, 53, 74

Egypt, 55, 56, 74
equites, 21–23, 34–37, 39, 41, 43, 48, 69, 72, 92

First Triumvirate, the, 41, 43, 47, 56, 57, 60, 67, 68, 85

Gaul, 33, 44, 56, 60, 62, 63, 65, 67, 68, 72, 84

Italy, 12, 32, 34, 36, 37, 49, 50, 52, 53, 59, 62, 71–74, 76, 83–85

law-courts, 15, 21, 26, 29, 39, 40, 57, 58
Lentulus (Catiline's lieutenant), 31–33
Lentulus (consul 57), 52, 55
Luca, 56–58, 65

Marius (Gaius Marius), 13, 94
Milo (Titus Annius Milo), 52, 55, 56, 60–62, 94
Mithridates, 22, 24, 36
Mutina, 84, 85

nobiles, 13, 25, 27, 34, 81, 92
novi homines (new men), 25–27, 92

Octavian (Gaius Octavius), 82, 84–87, 90, 94

optimates, 28, 29, 33, 35, 37, 38, 40, 43, 44, 56, 60, 62, 63, 65, 66, 70, 71, 73, 76, 82, 92

Plutarch, 12, 13, 16, 24, 44, 45, 48, 49, 53, 76, 79, 80, 82
Pompey (Gnaeus Pompeius Magnus), 19, 20, 22–24, 28, 35–49, 52–63, 65, 67–69, 71, 73, 74, 80, 94
populares, 27–30, 56, 92
praetorship (*praetor*), 22, 23, 32, 38, 40, 61, 63, 91
publicani (tax-collectors), 23, 24, 26, 39, 40, 43, 44, 69
quaestorship (*quaestor*), 18, 21, 91

Ravenna, 56, 70, 71
Rome, 12–15, 17–19, 21–24, 26, 28, 30–32, 35–37, 39, 40, 43, 44, 48–53, 58–68, 70, 76, 78, 79, 81–84, 86–88, 90
Rubicon, 71, 72

Senate, 13–18, 21–23, 28, 30–32, 34–37, 39–41, 43–45, 47, 52, 53, 56, 58, 62, 65, 67, 68, 70–74, 76, 78, 79, 81, 85, 86
Short Guide to Electioneering, 24–26
Sicily, 12, 18, 19, 21
Spain, 40, 49, 73, 77
Sulla (Lucius Cornelius Sulla), 14–17, 19, 21, 22, 62, 78, 87, 95

Terentia, 50, 51, 76, 82
tribunate (tribune), 14, 15, 19, 22, 23, 28, 40, 44, 45, 48, 52, 53, 66, 68, 69, 70, 71, 82, 92
Tullia, 50, 51, 53, 76, 82

Ultimate Decree of Senate, 30, 32, 70, 72

Verres, 21, 22, 64